Donald Trump Defeats The Deep State

Obama, Hillary
and
The Harlot

Will Clark

Donald Trump
Defeats
The Deep State

Published by
Motivation Basics
P.O. Box 6327
Diamondhead, MS 39525

Contents

Introduction

To many, the Book of Revelation is a document composed of many codes and puzzles too difficult to read and interpret. It begins by revealing letters written to the seven ancient churches in Asia, now known as the nation of Turkey. Some may ask why specific letters to those ancient churches would apply to a revelation of events today.

Other parts of the Book introduce and discuss horses, scorpions and locusts as if they were real animals representing some horrible monsters. Mixed in with these descriptions are discussions of earthquakes and great hail from the sky. Certainly a skeptic might ask what these things would have to do with prophesy and revelation. They might ask why the prophet John didn't write these prophesies in clear understandable words. There's a good reason John wrote his revelations in codes and analogies.

John's revelation was presented from Words and visions from Christ. Only the visions John saw were often written in codes and analogies because many of the things he saw were items and events he had never seen and certainly didn't know their names. In other places John used the words of stars, angels, and beasts to describe the result of an activity, a messenger or some connection. For example he used the analogy of the 'great star Wormwood that fell' to describe the rise of a major drug problem in the world. According to that verse, that bitter wormwood kills many people. Wormwood is a plant that produces bitter absinthe as well as artificial cannabis.

Many other analogies and metaphors are revealed as we read further into this book. But for now let's consider the beginning, the introduction of Revelation, that lays out the premise of John's message. His message is not to be deceived by false apostles and false Jews who would turn us from the Word of God and lead us into the hands of the one who has sworn to remove God's time from Heaven. He also cautions all believers to be prepared for that day when Christ will return to remove that evil who challenges Him for power. This warning is made very clear. So let's begin by demonstrating how and why those letters to the ancient Seven Churches are the beginning of the events taking place even today. It begins in Chapter 2 with the letter to the church at Ephesus, which begins with words of comfort:

"I know thy works, and thy labour, and thy patience, and how thou canst not bear them which are evil; and thou hast tried them which say they are apostles, and are not, and hast found them liars." Then after words of caution to repent for other matters he adds a common caution to all: "He that hath an ear, let him hear what the Spirit saith unto the churches."

The next letter is to the church as Smyrna. In that letter, He recognizes their works, tribulation, and poverty then adds, "I know the blasphemy of them which say they are Jews, and are not, but are the synagogue of Satan." He closes with that common caution, "He that hath and ear, let him hear what the Spirit saith unto the churches."

The letter to Pergamos is somewhat different. In the beginning He recognizes their faith, but then criticizes them for having those among them that "hold the doctrine of Balaam, who taught Balac to cast a stumbling block before the children of Israel, to eat things sacrificed unto idols, and to commit fornications." In this case, Balaam was an accepted prophet who was rewarded by Balac to cause the newly freed Jews to leave his nation, which they had occupied during their flight journey. Many of the newly freed Jews were destroyed when they followed that prophet into disaster. They were led away by that 'false' prophet. That same common caution ends the letter to Pergamos.

Again, He recognizes the good works of those in the church in Thyatira, then adds his displeasure, "Notwithstanding I have a few things against thee, because thou sufferest that woman Jezebel, which calleth herself a prophetess, to teach and to seduce my servants to commit fornication, and to eat things sacrificed unto idols." Then to use this Jezebel as the example for all false prophets and false Jews he explains further: "And I gave her space to repent of her fornication, and she repented not. Behold, I will cast her into a bed, and them that commit adultery with her into great tribulation except they repent of their deeds." Then verse 23 in Chapter 2 establishes the connection with the full story in Revelation:

"And I will kill her children with death, and all the churches shall know that I am he which searcheth the reins and hearts; and I will give unto every one of you according to your works." The common caution is then also added at the end of this letter; "He that hath an ear let him hear what the Spirit saith unto the churches."

This Jezebel of old is such a clear representation of the current Jezebel that we should explore further to understand. The current Jezebel of Revelation is identified as a 'woman' and as 'Babylon the Great.' This is the lynchpin code that offers clarity to Revelation. For more clarity it must be realized that this woman is one of only two described in Revelation. The goal of this Jezebel woman is to destroy that other identified woman, which is Christianity. This information about the Jezebel of old comes from Biography.com.

"Jezebel was a Phoenician princess who married Ahab, the prince of Israel. Eventually, they ruled as king and queen. Jezebel continued to worship the nature god Baal. Her citizens and the Yahweh prophet Elijah despised such actions. Preparing herself to be murdered by General Jehu, she applied makeup and dressed in finery before she was thrown over her balcony and eaten by dogs. Like Cleopatra, Jezebel's story is one of intrigue, romance and ultimately, the fall of a nation.

Queen of Israel: In 922 B.C., the nation of Israel was torn into two nations, Israel to the north and Judah to the south. Israel was racked by internal tribal differences and, subsequently, became susceptible to frequent invasions. It was, however, solidly following the beliefs of Yahweh, the "one and true" God, according to the Bible. Phoenicia (now known as Lebanon) was located to Israel's north, and on the whole, was just the opposite—cosmopolitan, populous and religiously diverse.

At the beginning of that century, a Phoenician princess named Jezebel was born, the daughter of King Ethball. The Bible does not describe her childhood, but from deductive reasoning, it is assumed that she lived in a fine home and was educated by the best tutors. Her family worshiped many gods, the most important being Baal, a nature god. While Jezebel was growing into a woman, Israel crowned a new king. To create an alliance with Israel, the king arranged for his son Ahab to wed Jezebel. Their marriage cemented a political alliance, but it was a dramatic event for the young woman. After enjoying a life of luxury, she was suddenly taken into a conservative society and made to oversee it.

Jezebel eventually became Israel's Queen. She continued to worship the god Baal, and in doing so, earned many enemies. Her citizens' displeasure came to a critical point when, at their expense, she brought 800 Baal prophets to Israel and ordered the murder of several Yahweh prophets. At this major moment, Elijah, a Jewish prophet, appeared. According to the biblical book of Kings, Elijah gave a prophecy: That terrible draught would come upon Israel. Amazingly, famine and draught spread across Jezebel's land, according to the story.

Final Years: The story of Naboth is perhaps the best-known story of Jezebel's life. Naboth, a common landowner who lived close to the King's residence, was asked to give his land to King Ahab in exchange for some compensation. Because of Jewish law, Naboth refused to give up his family's ancestral land. Incited by Naboth's refusal to King Ahab, Jezebel falsely charged him with treason and blaspheming "God and the king," and had him condemned to death by stoning. She then took his plot of land for the king. At this point,

Elijah arrived and confronted King Ahab about this brutal transgression, and then predicted that Ahab and all of his heirs would be killed and that dogs will eat Jezebel, according to the famous story.

Several years later, Ahab died in a battle against the Syrians, and a man named Jehu was promised the crown if he killed Jezebel's son, thus taking Jezebel's power. As the story goes, Jehu made his way to Jezebel's palace to murder her, and she, expecting him, applied make-up and dressed herself in finery. Her actions have been interpreted in a variety of ways—some people believe she was simply dressing for a dignified death. Others believe she was "painting" herself in hopes of seducing Jehu and becoming his mistress. In the end, she was thrown out of her bedroom window, trampled by horses and eaten by dogs."

In summary, this false prophetess led many Jews from God to worship her god, Baal. Many perished in the end. This is the same Jezebel who represents the religion that threatens to destroy God and his followers today. Presently there is only one religion that daily threatens to kill Jews and Christians; and in fact every day they are fulfilling that mission. They are the 'woman' who rides the 'scarlet colored beast' described in Chapter 17, verse 3. That scarlet colored beast is Satan himself. Revelation is the pure prophesy that warns the world to beware of false prophets, false Jews, and those who claim they are Jews but are not.

Beware of Jezebel; she is alive, active, and totally determined to entice others from the glory of God. When read individually and understood as a story the following articles give the total description and view of this Jezebel; this Babylon the Great.

Articles

Article 1
The Pope falls into Jezebel's Trap

On February 8, 2019 an article at Christiannews appeared with this title, 'Pope Francis, Islamic Imam Sign Declaration Calling for World Peace, 'Dialogue Among Believers.' This is a brief summary of that article:

"Jorge Bergoglio, also known as "Pope Francis," and Islamic Sheikh Ahmed al-Tayeb, the grand imam of Al Azhar, met together this week and signed a declaration calling for tolerance and peace among the nations of the world, as well as dialogue between the world's religions and cultures, which includes cooperation in tackling society's ills. The move has been questioned by some as being another step toward one world religion.

In speaking on the freedom of religion, it asserts that "the diversity of religions … are willed by God," and that men should not be "forced to adhere to a certain religion or culture."

As anyone with even a minute knowledge of Islam knows Islam's written goal is to be the only religion left on earth at the end of their great jihad. Their god, Satan, swore in Chapter 10 of Revelation to remove God from Heaven. Furthermore, Islam does not worship Jesus. They worship Muhammad and recognize Jesus as only a minor prophet such as Moses and Abraham. Verses 9-11 from Second John gives the warning against this:

"Whosoever transgresseth, and abideth not in the doctrine of Christ, hath not God. He that abideth in the doctrine of Christ, he hath both the Father and the Son. If there come any unto you, and bring not this doctrine, receive him not into your house, neither bid him God speed. For he that biddeth him God speed is partaker of his evil deeds."

Why has the Pope bid this satanic religion 'God speed?' Why has he invited him into the house of Christians?

An article by Heather Clark on February 8, 2019 explains further:

"According to Vatican News, the "Document on Human Fraternity for World Peace and Living Together" was signed on Monday in Abu Dhabi, and calls for "all persons who have faith in God and faith in human fraternity to unite and work together."

It also declares "in the name of God," and on behalf of those who identify as Muslim and Catholic, "the adoption of a culture of dialogue as the path; mutual cooperation as the code of conduct; reciprocal understanding as the method and standard."

"We, who believe in God and in the final meeting with Him and His judgment, on the basis of our religious and moral responsibility, and through this document, call upon ourselves, upon the leaders of the world as well as the architects of international policy and world economy, to work strenuously to spread the culture of tolerance and of living together in peace," the document states.

In speaking on the freedom of religion, it asserts that "the diversity of religions … are willed by God," and that men should not be "forced to adhere to a certain religion or culture."

"The pluralism and the diversity of religions, color, sex, race and language are willed by God in His wisdom, through which He created human beings," the document reads. "This divine wisdom is the source from which the right to freedom of belief and the freedom to be different derives. Therefore, the fact that people are forced to adhere to a certain religion or culture must be rejected, as too the imposition of a cultural way of life that others do not accept."

It additionally condemns violence in the name of religion, and urges the nations of the world to work together toward tolerance and peace. The declaration further touches on mutual beliefs about subjects such as protecting life, caring for the poor and elderly, and supporting the rights of women and children." End.

Article 2
Where is That Seat of Satan?

Do you remember that statement in John's letter in Revelation to the church in Pergamos (also called Pergamum): "I know thy works, and where thou dwellest, even where Satan's seat is?" There is a symbolic relic of Satan's seat still located there. It's part of a column that supported the Aesclepieion, a renowned medical center at that time. The Temple of Telesphorus, another god of medicine, was nearby.

The Aesclepieion was a healing center that never accepted critically ill people. Therefore a sign explained it's goal, 'Death may not enter here.' Telesphorus was the psychological part of the center and used snakes in dark tunnels as part of the treatments. The worshiped snakes in the tunnels and the adornment of the buildings represent that 'seat of Satan.'

Article 3
Free Stuff

In Paul's Second Letter to the Thessalonians he warned against not working to earn your own bread. Was this the earliest warning against 'free stuff and socialism?' Verses 7-12:

"For yourselves know how ye ought to follow us: for we behaved not ourselves disorderly among you; Neither did we eat any man's bread for nought; but wrought with labor and travail night and day, that we might not be chargeable to any of you; Not because we have not power, but to make ourselves an ensample (example) unto you to follow us. For even when we were with you, this we commanded you, that if any would not work, neither should he eat. For we hear that there are some which walk among you disorderly, working not at all, but are busybodies. Now them that are such we command and exhort by our Lord Jesus Christ, that with quietness they work, and eat their own bread."

Isn't it amazing and terrible how many people today follow the distorted and blasphemous words of those who promote Satan's path to sadness and self destruction? This is happening today as Democrats promise their followers free bread and other free stuff in return for their votes that will put them in power to give more free stuff. Those who hope for, vote for, and wait for all that free stuff will never achieve those heights which are much more important; happiness and salvation.

By not striving for personal success and happiness they will never get anywhere or contribute anything to humanity. Those who reach their goals of happiness and success are fully aware that the most important thing with which to begin one's life is a job. From there anything is possible, even great happiness and a feeling of enriched fulfillment. Earning is contributing and giving; waiting for free stuff is taking without a goal or a purpose.

Article 4

Why Have Walls?

The Democrats who once supported walls and the concept of security now say walls are immoral. Does that mean Democrats were immoral before and now are seeking God's Grace through new-found morality? If that's what they claim then they are perpetrating the greatest deception in world history.

Some of the things they proclaim to support their position are true. It's true that walls will not stop all illegal immigration, drugs, and gang members from coming into America. But a wall does serve a higher purpose than those ideas submitted by Democrats.

First, walls do protect those who protect us on this side of the wall. Have you ever seen the Arizona desert south of Interstate 8 as it flows below Tucson and Casa Grande? It's a barren area where our Border Patrol and other protectors can easily be ambushed and killed trying to defend our nation. An Iranian book celebrating suicide bombers, "In Memory of Our Martyrs," was found there in 2011. A wall in those barren areas focuses invaders into areas more easily controlled.

But, a wall or a barrier serves an even greater purpose than that. A wall gives a great statement of our honor and freedom. It symbolizes the idea that our forefathers sacrificed for us to create a nation of godly patriots, not a nation that would allow itself to be destroyed by those invited to come in to destroy that godly foundation. This is the hope of those Democrats who proudly invite those in to destroy our destiny. Perhaps Second Timothy 3:1-5, gives a clue as to the basis and aim of those Democrats:

"This know also, that in the last days perilous times shall come. For men shall be lovers of their own selves, covetous, boasters, proud, blasphemers, disobedient to parents, unthankful, unholy, without natural affection, trucebreakers, false accusers, incontinent, fierce, despisers of those that are good, traitors, heady, highminded, lovers of pleasures more than lovers of God; Having a form of godliness, but denying the power thereof: from such turn away."

Many haughty voices of traitors, blasphemers, and despisers of those that are good are trying to destroy our current protector. May God continue to bless and guide President Trump to protect us.

Article 5

Babylon the Great Dances in the Street

There's an article on Face Book suggesting that America is that Babylon the Great described in Revelation. Although the writer probably means well his conclusion is totally wrong. That Babylon the Great introduced in Revelation is the Islamic religion.

In verse 3 of Chapter 17 an angel is explaining a vision to Apostle John. It identifies and describes a woman (religion) riding a scarlet colored beast 'full of names of blasphemy.' That beast is the red dragon, Satan. Then verse 5 adds to the description of that woman, "And upon her forehead was a name written, Mystery, Babylon the Great, the Mother of Harlots and Abominations of the Earth." Then in verse 6 John explains the identity of the woman (religion):

"And I saw the woman drunken with the blood of the saints, and with the blood of the martyrs of Jesus." No other religion (woman) on God's great Earth, except Islam, is drunken with the blood of Christians and Jews. They even celebrate and exchange gifts when certain Christians and Jews are killed; such as they did when many were killed during the 9-11 horror. Many Islamists even danced in the streets. This is a clear and definitive description. Islam is that Babylon who rides (worships) their god, Satan.

Article 6
Metaphors of Babylon the Great.

In a recent article I tried to describe a time line that helped explain many metaphors and analogies in John's Revelation. Since John didn't know the names of things and events that were to occur centuries later, he used metaphors coupled with a time to explain the event. In this case the time line was described as 'time, times, and half a time.' He used this clue from one given in Daniel over 500 years before. In Chapter 12, verses 6-7, when Daniel asked "How long shall it be to the end of these wonders" a man clothed in linen answered, "– it shall be for a time, times, and an half." The man didn't say how many years or what the event would be; but the time gives a clue.

It wouldn't be three and a half years (1+2+1/2.) It wouldn't be 350 years; for nothing significant happened during those time frames. So let's examine 3500 years. Could that be the time of that great war of Gog and Magog which will end the thousand years of peace after Armageddon? (Revelation 20:7-10) If that's the case, then Armageddon must not be far away. Understanding that times are approximate (500BC+2000+1000 = 3500.)

John also gave a more specific clue in Revelation. The beginning of Chapter 12 describes the birth of Christianity from a 'man child' described in verse 5. Verse 6 describes the family's flight to Egypt for protection from Herod; where they stayed for 'a thousand two hundred and threescore days,' or three and a half years.

Christians continued to be persecuted for another 350 years which ended with Rome's adoption of Christianity through actions of Constantine the Great after he reunited Rome. Verse 14 describes the woman (Christianity) being protected by 'two wings of a great eagle' for a time, times, and half a time. Rome is represented by an eagle with great wings. That protection ended after another 350 years, which brings the time line to 700 AD. What happened then? Islam was created and immediately began attacking and killing all Christians and Jews.

The chapter concludes by stating that the dragon "was wroth with the woman, and went to make war with the remnant of her seed, which keep the commandments of God, and have the testimony of Jesus Christ." Yes, Islam is creating murder and mayhem still today. Their horror is now so bad that Islam is considered by Apostle John as 'Babylon the Great.'

Article 7

Bleeding Hearts or Heartless Robbers?

If you think sanctuary cities and sanctuary states are acting as sanctuary out of the 'goodness of their hearts' think again. We all know it's a ploy to gain votes to grasp more socialist power, but there's also a more immediate purpose for their deception. Their immediate purpose, if they can maintain enough power with those ill-gained and false votes, is to increase revenue and taxes in their states and cities.

I began to wonder about this when I remembered the concept from my college Banking class that money ordinarily turns over 7 times in a community. So, I searched the source of welfare programs under, 'How Are Welfare Programs Funded in the United States.' This was the answer:

"In the United States, the various programs comprising the country's welfare system are primarily funded by the federal government. The six main programs of the U.S. social welfare structure include Temporary Assistance for Needy Families, Supplemental Security Income, the Food Stamp Program, Earned Income Tax Credit, Medicaid and Housing Assistance."

Now consider how even illegal immigrants spend that free money. Every item they buy is taxed with a sales tax. The seller is taxed with a state tax. Sellers pay tax when they buy something with the money paid to them by those illegals. It goes on and on and continues to compound revenue for those sanctuary cities and states, while regular citizens are taxed more.

Those 'bleeding heart' areas care absolutely nothing about the welfare and safety of their invaders. They care only about taking our hard-earned tax dollars for themselves and their communities. Perhaps our federal government should expose this robbery conspiracy.

<h1 style="text-align:center">Article 8</h1>

Is Revelation Worth Reading?

Is it important to read and understand the Book of Revelation? Chapter 1, verse 3 gives the answer: "Blessed is he that readeth, and they that hear the words of this prophecy , and keep those things which are written therein: for the time is at hand." These specific words led me to study Revelation almost daily for at least the past five years. Almost all my books within that time are based on the words and descriptions in Revelation. Many of these books are free.

Many believe Revelation is about unbelievable monsters and events; therefore they avoid the words believing they are from Apostle John's fantastic imagination. In reality, it gives a clear story with pictures, like reading a complicated novel. Two examples are of time and events.

The time of the coming great disaster where God will have had enough of Satan's attack on His realm and humanity and will take action to destroy this evil; Islam being Satan's worldly physical force. For the first time clue we divert to Second Timothy, Chapter 3:

"This know also, that in the last days perilous times shall come. For men shall be lovers of their own selves, covetous, boasters, proud, blasphemers, disobedient to parents, unthankful, unholy, without natural affection, trucebreakers, false accusers, incontinent, fierce, despisers of those that are good, traitors, heady, highminded, lovers of pleasures more than lovers of God; Having a form of godliness, but denying the power thereof: from such turn away." Can anyone deny that this condition is taking place now, today?

The second time clue is in Revelation, Chapter 8, regarding a great star Wormwood coming down to earth. This star represents an event;

that event being the great disaster caused by drugs. The bitterness refers to the plant wormwood which is the source of the bitter drink absinthe. Now let's analyze the events represented by 'great monsters.'

Chapter 9 is the great source of fright that keeps many from analyzing Revelation. It refers to locusts, scorpions, teeth of lions and other great horrors. Anyone who has been in a war zone, such as I was in Vietnam in 1967, these are easy to decipher. Those 'locusts' John saw were aircraft on the horizon. John didn't know to call them airplanes. Those scorpions are helicopters. John didn't know that word so he described them by appearance. Yes, they are shaped like scorpions. Those teeth like teeth of lions were the grills on battle vehicles such as tanks. The 'hair of women' described women John saw participating in combat. Every metaphor in Chapter 9 has a logical explanation. John didn't know the modern words to describe what he saw in his visions.

Perhaps Chapter 1, verse 3 is a very important guide for those who believe and are concerned. It might even be urgent considering the growing hostility taking place at the moment against Israel.

Article 9

Is that Beast Sneaking in the Back Door?

As most of us are aware, our nation and the world are now going through 'troubling times' which is one of the warnings in Revelation of the tribulation to come. The answer to when that will happen is not given definitely, but we do have clues to that beginning time when Christ will appear to remove that beast causing all these frustrations and anger in the world and in our great nation. America has never been so angry within. That beast is gaining more hearts and minds in his realm to challenge the Goodness of God. That beast leads his blasphemous army of Islam.

Daniel, Chapter 9, verse 27 gives the first clue. It identifies a covenant for seven years that will be abandoned 'in the midst.' Certainly this must refer to Obama's Iran agreement. It was made in July, 2015; so 'in the midst' could be any time after this April.

Another clue is the identification and information about the 'second beast,' that false prophet identified in Chapter 13. It begins by saying he had the same power as the first beast. That first beast was Muhammad. Then verse 15 adds, "And he had power to give life unto the image of the beast, that the image of the beast should both speak, and cause that as many as would not worship the image of the beast should be killed."

Obama was the leader of a nation, the same power as was Muhammad. Obama helped create ISIS which is the 'image of that beast, Islam.' Furthermore, Obama gave the beast even more power by giving them 150 billion dollars to continue supporting Satan's army against Christ.

But now what's the latest clue? It's a reference to distraction, which will allow a surprise attack. Chapter 16, verse 15, "Behold, I come as a thief. Blessed is he that watcheth, and keepeth his garments, lest he walk naked, and they see his shame." With all the hate and distraction in the world today, especially the determined hateful actions against Donald Trump in our nation, no one is watching the greatest threat to the world; that beast, Iran, and it's attack against Israel.

That beast, Islam and Iran, is likely sneaking toward the back door even now to attack Israel. Perhaps personal precautions are in order at this very minute for those who understand.

Article 10
Will There be War with Islam?

I have written about this several times already, but I believe a critical time approaches that should concern us deeply. The crucial questions are: Who is Babylon the Great? Will there be a war with Babylon the Great? Who will win that Great Battle?

Verses 5-6 in Revelation, Chapter 17 answers the first question with the understanding that 'woman, she, and her' refer to a religion. Two religions are described in Revelation. Chapter 12 introduces and describes Christianity; while 17 describes Islam. It begins, "And upon her forehead was a name written, MYSTERY BABYLON THE GREAT, THE MOTHER OF HARLOTS AND ABOMINATIONS OF THE EARTH. And I saw the woman drunken with the blood of the saints and with the blood of the martyrs of Jesus."

Verse 14 continues to answer the next two questions, "These shall make war with the Lamb, and the Lamb shall overcome them: for he is Lord of lords, and King of kings. Chapter 18, verses 2-3 add, "And he cried mightily with a strong voice, saying, 'Babylon the great is fallen, is fallen, and is become the habitation of devils, and the hold of every foul spirit, and a cage of every unclean and hateful bird. For all nations have drunk of the wine of the wrath of her fornication, and the kings of the earth have committed fornication with her.'

Babylon the Great, Islam, will also kill one another as they are doing at this very moment. Chapter 6, verse 4 explains this detail, "And there went out another horse that was red: and power was given to him that sat thereon (Islam) to take peace from the earth, and that they should kill one another; and there was given unto him a great sword." Doesn't this clearly describe what's happening in the Muslim countries today?

The Great Question is: will it happen suddenly with a big bomb, or will it creep slowly with larger encroachments? No doubt, however, it seems to be very near.

Article 11

The Codes of Revelation

For those who read Revelation and wonder if there really is a clear and definite message within, don't despair. The message is a true prophesy; and many of the events recorded are becoming clearer every passing day. Most likely, Apostle John knew the interpretation would be difficult but he had to write much of it in code to prevent his captors, the Romans, from destroying his writing while he was exiled on the Island of Patmos. Perhaps the greatest codes of interpretation he gave us was of 'time, times, and half a time' and 'two wings of a great eagle,' in Chapter 12.

He established the time Jesus was in Egypt, 'a thousand, two hundred and threescore days,' (3 and a half years) as an equation of 1+2+1/2. Using that equation and beginning with the time Jesus returned to Israel, he identified the time Christianity was protected by 'two wings of a great eagle' (Rome) beginning approximately 350 AD. (Verse 14.) At the end of that time, another 350 years, Christianity was again attacked by the serpent. That was approximately 700 AD, which is the beginning of Islam. Verse 17 then explains the continuing attack against Christians and Jews since that time - even today:

"And the dragon was wroth with the woman (Christianity) and went to make war with the remnant of her seed, which keep the commandments of God, and have the testimony of Jesus Christ."

Chapters 12, 13, and 17 have very clear messages with similar coding. Basically Chapter 12 describes the arrival of Christianity; with Satan determined to destroy her as soon as she was born. Chapter 13 gives clear definitions of Satan, the beast (antichirst) and the second beast (false prophet.) Chapter 17 gives a clear vision of Islam and the deceptions of Islam.

Article 12
Earth Ends in Twelve Years?

More Democrats are jumping on the bandwagon raising more flags that because of uncontrolled global warming the world will end in twelve years. Bernie Sanders even raised this flag again during the recent Democrat debates. Their sobbing plea has nothing to do with protecting our earth or our citizens. It has everything to do with gaining personal socialistic power through the creation of a one-world order with themselves at the top to control how we live. They want total autocracy for themselves to control our personal day-to-day lives. They care nothing for our happiness, safety or security even at the expense of inviting Biblical disaster.

Since it's certain that the Bible has more credibility and Truth than those deceptive and blasphemous words coming from the mouths of Democrats let's see what the Bible has to say about those twelve years. The Bible is very clear and truthful.

Revelation, Chapter 20, verses 4-9 explains that the next war after Armageddon will not occur for a thousand years. That thousand years is commonly referred to as the Millennium. At the end of that time (verse 8) will come the 'Gog and Magog' war. After that will be a reckoning that will result in 'a new heaven and a new earth.' (Chapter 21, first verse.)

Armageddon has not happened yet, but with the Democrats splitting our national resolve to be a 'one nation under God' it's possible that Iran could attack Israel at any time; thereby creating the condition to begin that great war. Iran is sitting on the sidelines watching and waiting until they feel the Democrats have destroyed Donald Trump's influence enough that they can safely attack. With their nation now failing what do they have to lose? At the right moment they will sneak in 'like a thief in the night.'

No; the earth absolutely will not end in 'twelve years.'

Article 13

Who is Babylon the Great?

Who is Babylon the Great? Revelation 17:5 presents a description: "And upon her forehead was a name written, Mystery Babylon the Great, the Mother of Harlots and Abominations of the Earth." This question has been a mystery since Apostle John wrote the Book of Revelation two thousand years ago.

Some claim Babylon is the Vatican. They even write that the Pope as head of that religion is the prophesied Antichrist. Still many others write that the United States will become that prophesied Babylon with her fall from grace and economics; which will lead to degradation and turning from God in despair.

Throughout history many have offered a definition of this Babylon; but in vain. The mystery of this question could not have been solved until our current generation. Now that answer is 'crystal clear' as prophesied in Revelation 4:6. The mystery is solved in the verse following the one describing Mystery Babylon. Verse 6 continues:

"And I saw the woman drunken with the blood of the saints and with the blood of the martyrs of Jesus."

Only two religions are described as women in Revelation. One is Christianity. The other is represented by Babylon the Great; the whore that sits upon the scarlet colored beast. Babylon is revealed. She still rides that scarlet colored beast called Satan; and she still delights in destroying Christians and anything related to the Grace of God. Yes; Babylon is that religion; and she is hell-bound to create such havoc and chaos on earth until that Great War erupts. But even with her great strength given by Satan she will be defeated and totally annihilated as praised by an angel in Chapter 18: "Babylon the Great is fallen, is fallen!"

God's forces will win that Great Battle as described in Chapter 9. That battle will begin when the fifth angel sounds the fifth trumpet. God's forces will be led by a king, 'the angel of the bottomless pit' whose name in Greek is Apollyon. This is described as 'Destroyer.' Could the sound of the fifth 'trumpet' announce the arrival of a king named Trump who will act in the Spirit of Christ to defeat this great horror?

At this moment in time of Satan's great threats Donald Trump is the only leader who expresses the God-given resolve and ambition to protect the world from Satan's great evil. He continues and perseveres in the Spirit while other 'great leaders' and media continue trying to destroy him. Are those trying to destroy him guided by those six angels removed from Heaven with Satan when he was removed by Michael and his angels?

Article 14
Warriors for Christ

Isn't Bible prophesy absolutely amazing? It even answers the question about whether an evil person can be chosen to lead the battle to preserve or restore God's will and Christianity. Revelation answers this question clearly and precisely.

The first example is Emperor Constantine's conquest at the Battle at Milvian Bridge in 312 AD to reunite Rome. Due to Constantine's vision before the battle he had his men paint the Christian cross on their shields. Until then he was a pagan who worshiped the sun god and persecuted Christians as did other Romans. Christians and Jews were then accepted as equal citizens of Rome; and were protected by that 'two wings of a great eagle' for 350 years. (Time, times, and half a time: Revelation, Chapter 12, verse 14.) Constantine was known as Constantine the Great. An eagle with great wings is the symbol of Rome. Christians and Jews were again persecuted beginning approximately 700 AD with the rise of the Ottoman Empire - Muslims.

Chapter 9 describes a great war, likely the Battle of Armageddon. The war results from the bottomless pit (warfare.) Many misinterpret the 'angel of the bottomless pit' (abyss) as the antichrist or his representative. That is false. This person is the one who will lead that battle against Satan's forces. Verse 11 describes him as a king 'whose name is Abaddon or Apollyon.' A definition is given as 'destroyer or place of destruction.' Isn't it interesting that those who hate Donald Trump so deeply are already calling him a 'destroyer?'

Article 15
War and Triulation

This information is taken and interpreted from three Bible sources: Daniel, Chapter 9; Matthew, Chapter 24; and Revelation. It concerns difficult times coming our way that I interpret as very soon. That time of difficulty is identified as the tribulation period.

In Daniel it says that a covenant will be made by many nations regarding the protection of Israel. And, in the 'midst' of that seven year covenant it will be abandoned and Israel will be attacked. Matthew gives more information about this sudden and vicious attack and how to be ready. This certainly must refer to that Iran Nuclear Agreement made in July, 2015. No other covenant in history was ever made by multiple nations, seven in this agreement, regarding the protection of Israel. The tribulation will be for seven years and the great tribulation will be the last half of that seven years. We are now nearing the midst of Obama's Iran nuclear covenant.

Barack Obama was the architect of that covenant and he is also the 'second beast' in Revelation who allowed that image to the beast to be created. In other words he facilitated and assisted the growth of ISIS which is the caliphate image to the Muslim beast created by the first beast; the antichrist Muhammad. This is that image 'to' the beast, not 'of' the beast mentioned in Revelation, Chapter 13. This image of the beast is interpreted by many to be some computer generated image that speaks. It's the ISIS caliphate.

The third clue to the nearing of the attack against Israel is from Revelation, Chapter 8, with the introduction of a Great star named Wormwood that will harm and kill many people just before that great attack. Wormwood is a synonym of the great drug problem the world faces today. It's that time.

Now Hamas and others are positioning more missiles and rockets toward Israel, and Iran is testing more of their rockets. I don't think they are doing these offensive tactics just to see a great fireworks display. Perhaps the leaders of the world should take more seriously what these followers of Satan are really doing. And it's not a surprise. Iran states openly and boldly that they will destroy Israel. With the world in immigration chaos and the Democrats viciously attacking Donald Trump every minute and every hour, what better time is there for Iran's sudden attack?

Additional Information:

Matthew 24:22, "And except those days should be shortened, there should no flesh be saved: but for the elect's sake those days shall be shortened."

2 Timothy 3:1-5, "This know also, that in the last days perilous times shall come. For men shall be lovers of their own selves, covetous, boasters, proud, blasphemers, disobedient to parents, unthankful, unholy, without natural affection, trucebreakers, false accusers, incontinent, fierce, despisers of those that are good, traitors, heady, highminded, lovers of pleasures more than lovers of God; Having a form of godliness, but denying the power thereof: from such turn away."

Matthew 24:37-39, "But as the days of Noah were, so shall also the coming of the Son of man be. For as in the days that were before the flood they were eating and drinking, marrying and giving in marriage, until the day that Noah entered into the ark, and knew not until the flood came, and took them all away; so shall also the coming of the Son of man be."

Article 16
He That Hath an Ear

In Revelation Apostle John writes letters to the seven churches of Asia. In reality from the Words given, this information is to all Christians of all time, including our time of today. When the Words are condensed and assimilated the letter to each church issues the same caution; that is not to be deceived by another force that will cause you to turn away from God's real church.

The caution at the end of each letter is the same, "He that hath an ear, let him hear what the Spirit saith unto the churches." In summary, He cautions against a woman named Jezebel who will lead many astray 'to commit fornication and to eat things sacrificed unto Idols.' (Chapter 2, verse 20.) This Jezebel and the other distractions identified to the churches are the composite of Islam. Then His Words in Chapter 12 reinforce this conclusion.

Several verses in Chapter 12 offer a definitive code to reinforce this conclusion that Islam is that beast who will attack God and those who worship God and Christ. That code is 'time, times, and half a time.'

Chapter 12 introduces a woman (religion) with 12 stars which represent the apostles. When a 'man child' is born he is immediately threatened with death and the family flees to safety (Egypt) where they remain for 'a thousand two hundred and threescore days.' This represents three and a half years, or one year plus two years plus a half year; time and times and half a time. (Verses 4-6) This is the key that unlocks the code.

When she (Christianity) returned she was persecuted under Rome for 350 years (time, and times and half a time.) Then Rome under Constantine (two wings of a great eagle, verse 14) protected and adopted Christianity for another time, times and half a time. This put the time line at approximately 700 AD. This was the time of the great rise of Islam and the invasion of most of the Roman Empire. Christians, Jews and many others were then under attack and slaughtered by the Muslim hoards. Verse 17 then reveals the results since the time of that initial invasion by Islam:

"And the dragon (the source of worship of Islam) was wroth with the woman, and went to make war with the remnant of her seed, which keep the commandments of God, and have the testimony of Jesus Christ." We Christians are the 'remnant of her seed.'

With these definitive codes of names and times revealed how can anyone doubt the validity of the prophesy of Revelation. This prophesy was written 2000 years ago; 350 years before Constantine, and 700 years before Muhammad established Islam. How can anyone today doubt the power of God or the prophesy of Christ? Yet many in our nation and world are now trying to destroy God's influence on humanity. We should not disregard His many warnings: "He that hath an ear, let him hear what the Spirit saith unto the churches."

Article 17
Who is the Antichrist?

In First John, Chapter 2, verse 18, John asks, "Little children, it is the last time: and as ye have heard that antichrist shall come. Even now are there many antichrists, whereby we know that it is the last time."

In his Second Letter, verses 9-11, John gives more information, "Whosoever transgresseth, and abideth not in the doctrine of Christ, hath not God. He that abideth in the doctrine of Christ, he hath both the Father and the Son. If there come any unto you, and bring not this doctrine, receive him not into your house, neither bid him God speed. For he that bideth him God speed is partaker of his evil deeds."

This is critical information to identify the antichrist. First, he does not accept Christ as the Son of God. Muhammad led his followers in this belief. Islam does profess there is one named Jesus; they call him Isa, but consider him only a minor prophet such as Moses. Furthermore, Muhammad committed great blasphemy by being accepted as the only prophet near to God. In effect, he allowed himself to be considered in the place of Christ. Revelation, Chapter 13, verse 6 confirms this blasphemy, "And he opened his mouth in blasphemy against God, to blaspheme his name, and his tabernacle, and them that dwell in Heaven."

Then there are two other verses in Chapter 13 that clearly identify Muhammad as THE antichirst. Verse 3: "And I saw one of his heads as it were wounded to death, and his deadly wound was healed." This occurred as Muhammad led his troops in the Battle of Uhud in 624 AD. Verse 5 adds, "and power was given to him to continue forty and two months. He was poisoned in 628 AD and died in 632; three and a half years later.

Followers of this antichrist, Muhammad, are racing into our great nation now to destroy those of us who accept Christ as the Son of God. Their purpose, as assisted and promoted by that Second Beast, Barack Obama, is to destroy our nation; one nation under God. Now the Democrats are so desperate for power and control of our nation they are even assisting Muhammad and Obama in that deadly process. I will define Obama's role as the second beast in my next post.

Article 18

Who is That Second Beast?

In my last post I wrote that I would reveal Obama's role as that second beast, also called the false prophet in Revelation. This is that information.

To begin, it's urgent to realize that in Revelation the word 'beast' has several meanings. The four beasts in Chapters 4 and 6 are representations from God who have certain characteristics that allow them to introduce the 'four horses' of the Apocalypse. For example, the fourth beast 'was like a flying eagle,' which represented his world view to introduce the pale horse that would bring horror and pestilence over the entire world. The other beasts are different.

The other three beasts revealed in Chapter 13 are those who support Satan's plan to war against God. Satan's plan is revealed in Chapter 10, as 'a mighty angel who came down from Heaven.' These three beasts are Satan's army of Islam, the first beast (antichrist) Muhammad, and the second beast (false prophet) Barack Obama; from my analysis and conclusion. The first beast is also simply referred to as the 'beast,' the one who created Islam.

The death of that first beast, the antichrist, is given in verse 10, 'he that killeth with the sword must be killed with the sword.' Then the identity of the second beast begins in verse 11, "And I beheld another beast coming up out of the earth; (this means he is from this world not an angel from Heaven) and he had two horns like a lamb, and he spake as a dragon." This reference to the lamb indicates he claims to be of Christ, but his words were all to support that dragon, Satan. In this case that Satan is the leader and base of Islam. Islam is 'the beast.'

Verse 13 says he will create wonders (deception) by making fire 'come down from heaven on the earth in the sight of men.' When John wrote this he didn't know about aircraft and air power that Obama used to deceptively claim to be fighting against ISIS and other Muslim terrorist organizations. Verse 15 adds that he had power to give life to that image of the beast, which is that Islamic caliphate.

Verse 12 states that he had the same power as the first beast which means he was the leader of a nation, as was Muhammad. Only one man fulfills this prophesy. That man is Barack Hussein Obama. The number of letters in his name also fulfills the prophesy in verse 18 of 'count the number of the beast which is the number of a man. His number is 666.' Counting 666 gives a total of the number 18: BARACKHUSSEINOBAMA. Isn't it ironic that this information is confirmed by being in verse 18.

Article 19
Danger Through the Back Door

Democrats inviting terrorists and other illegals into our nation to destroy the identity of our great nation reminds me of a traitorous Greek in ancient history. His name was Ephialtes and he aided the Persian King Xerxes in his attack against the 'Spartan 300' at the Thermopylae Pass in 480 BC.

Persia, now Iran, was a dominating power at that time along with the powerful Greeks. Little known is that Persian King Xerxes was the son of King Darius and the son-in-law of King Cyrus. King Darius succeeded Nebucanezzar after his destruction of Jerusalem. Darius was the king who assigned Daniel to the lions' den then appointed Daniel to a high position when Daniel survived. Darius and Cyrus are mentioned in the Book of Daniel.

King Cyrus destroyed the ancient city of Sardis, one of the seven churches of Revelation. Sardis was located on a river flecked with gold. At that time Croesus, the richest man in the world, was the king of Sardis, obviously based on the riches he gathered from that river.

This created the saying 'rich as Croesus.' On the way to his execution Croesus was spared by King Cyrus due to a dream. Now, what about this traitor Ephialtes?

The leader of the Spartans, Leonidas, refused to allow Ephialtes to help guard the narrow Thermopylae Pass due to his weakness. During the great battle where the small number of Spartans stood their ground (The Spartan 300) against thousands of Persians the traitor guided the rear of the Persian army through a narrow hidden pass to the rear of the Spartans. The Spartans were helpless from the rear and were defeated.

Isn't this similar to Democrats refusing to help defend America because Hillary Clinton was defeated for president; and they are inviting our enemies to harm us through the 'back door?' Democrats are refusing to help our elected president, Donald Trump, defend America. Is their refusal to help build our defenses, including a wall, the same as the traitor who led the Persian army through the back door to destroy the Spartans?

Are they offended by Donald Trump as Ephialtes was 'offended' by Leonidas? A traitor is a traitor regardless of his name or his purpose. It seems the Democrats are inviting our enemies to attack us through the back door for a vengeful purpose, not for the benefit of our great nation. Isn't their refusal to support defenses for our nation similar to the action by Ephialtes? It demonstrates a total disregard for the safety and security of our great nation. What would they do if one of them became president, whose prime responsibility is to enforce the safety and security of our nation?

Article 20
Satan's Sound is Blaring Today

Perhaps one of the greatest mysteries and prophesies in the Bible is in Revelation, Chapter 10. This short chapter explains a time when 'a mighty angel' will come down from Heaven and challenge God. This angel, Satan, even lifts up his hands and swears that God's time in Heaven will be ended, 'that there should be time no longer.' Since six other angels accompanied Satan when he was removed from Heaven by Michael and his angels Satan is regarded as the seventh angel. It seems the prophesy of this seventh angel is being fulfilled today as given in verse 7. Verse 7!:

"But in the days of the voice of the seventh angel, when he shall begin to sound, the mystery of God should be finished, as he hath declared to his servants the prophets."

Satan also had a 'little book' in his hand that was 'sweet as honey in the mouth but bitter in the belly.' History suggests what this little book is and how it became the voice of that seventh angel. It was offered to Muhammad 'as he contemplated' in the Cave of Hira. It now guides the actions of Satan's great army Islam. Islam is not only 'sounding' for Satan today, Muslims are even shouting their determination to destroy God, to remove God's time from Heaven, from every roof top; even from the halls of our Congress. Yes, even many of our elected lawmakers have joined this great battle to destroy God's time in Heaven.

We have been warned. How prepared are we to reject the words of that false prophet?

Article 21
Fair Share and Free Everything

What a fantastic life to look forward to as a Democrat; in other words, as a Socialist traitor who wants to destroy our great nation. But what is their plan to pay for all these FREE things? It's simple; just tax those who have more than they really need, even up to 90 percent of what they earn. And if that leaves them with more than their fair share just tax it at 100 percent. Or as the wild young thing, our new congresswoman, exclaims, "Just pay for it!" But what would happen to the poor if Democrats (Socialists-Communists) were to have their way? Those who expect more fair share would have less and become totally destitute and horrified at their conditions.

If the rich have less to invest then the poor and middle class could not get loans to buy a house or a car - not even a bike. Carpenters and other builders would not have jobs. Without those jobs and others to buy things like food and clothing many other stores and businesses would be forced to close - putting even more people out of jobs creating even more destitution. Then the few things left on the grocery shelves would be too expensive for anyone to buy. Can you imagine a jar of peanut butter, if you could find one at a grocery store, costing fifty dollars or even more? Today, Venezuela is the perfect example of this self-destructive process; this distribution of a fair share.

Our system of Capitalism is designed for those more successful to earn more so the excess can be used to the highest and best advantage to maintain a civil and prosperous society. The more illegal immigrants the Democrats try to force into our nation the greater will be the disaster when those who despise our FREE way of life have their way. This is what they offer.

Under Capitalism one may aspire to personal success for self and family. Under Socialism one may aspire only to survive day to day without any thoughts of the future. Where do they think those loans for a house and car come from; and where do they think that financing of cans of food on grocery shelves comes from? Without some having excess funds to invest in others then those who are most poor would be unable to have anything. This is what the Democrats are offering; this is why Venezuela is in such turmoil today. The government has robbed the rich of providing support for those most poor. If the rich don't have enough to invest, then how the hell does the poor have support to survive?

Article 22

Beginning the Fair Share War

Many wonder what's the source behind the current force to destroy our nation by infiltrating Islam (the Silent Jihad) or by Socialism. I believe it's a deceptive plan orchestrated by the one I conclude is that 'second beast,' The description of that second beast is given in Revelation, Chapter 13, verses 11-14. These verses reveal that he claims to be a Christian but he speaks words of the dragon, Satan (Islam) and he influences by deception. This describes Barack Hussein Obama. These are the words that commit himself to that plan of destruction:

As President Obama has said, the change we seek will take longer than one term or one presidency. Real change—big change—takes many years and requires each generation to embrace the obligations and opportunities that come with the title of Citizen.

"True democracy is a project that's much bigger than any one of us. It's bigger than any one person, any one president, and any one government. It's a job for all of us."

Obama is now the leading force behind a growing group called Organizing for Action. Hidden in the background this group is focused on 'changing' America. It seems that in their lust for more extreme power the Democrats, especially Pelosi and Schumer, have turned their eyes from the things that will defend and protect our nation and our way of life. Their blind eyes do not see or understand Obama's satanic scheme.

Article 23
The Snake

These are the lyrics of 'The Snake' that Donald Trump has quoted several times. It refers to accepting those into our nation whose only goal and purpose is to destroy our nation.

The Snake Lyrics:

On her way to work one morning
Down the path along side the lake
A tender hearted woman saw a poor half frozen snake
His pretty colored skin had been all frosted with the dew
"Oh well," she cried, "I'll take you in and I'll take care of you"
"Take me in oh tender woman
Take me in, for heaven's sake
Take me in oh tender woman, " sighed the snake

She wrapped him up all cozy in a curvature of silk
And then laid him by the fireside with some honey and some milk
Now she hurried home from work that night as soon as she arrived
She found that pretty snake she'd taking in had been revived
"Take me in, oh tender woman
Take me in, for heaven's sake
Take me in oh tender woman, " sighed the snake

Now she clutched him to her bosom, "You're so beautiful," she cried
"But if I hadn't brought you in by now you might have died"
Now she stroked his pretty skin and then she kissed and held him
tight
But instead of saying thanks, that snake gave her a vicious bite
"Take me in, oh tender woman
Take me in, for heaven's sake
Take me in oh tender woman, " sighed the snake

"I saved you," cried that woman
"And you've bit me even, why?
You know your bite is poisonous and now I'm going to die"
"Oh shut up, silly woman," said the reptile with a grin

"You knew damn well I was a snake before you took me in

"Take me in, oh tender woman

Take me in, for heaven's sake

Take me in oh tender woman, " sighed the snake.

Songwriters: ROBERT S. KELLY, DARIAN MORGAN

Universal Music Publishing Group

https://www.youtube.com/watch?v=fHIcVuqQgVo

Article 24

Angels Sounding

Satan is identified as the 'seventh angel' in Revelation, Chapter 10. How do we know this seventh angel is Satan? Who are the other six?

It begins in the first verse of Chapter 12, where a woman (the religion Christianity) came down from heaven with a crown of twelve stars. This 12 represents Christ's apostles; two-thirds of the stars. Then Satan drew a third of the stars of Heaven with him when he was removed from Heaven. A third of the total of 18 stars would be 6 stars, which represent angels. Including his six angels, Satan would be the seventh angel.

Then the first verse in Chapter 13 begins to explain the rise of those seven angels and their war against God. "And I stood upon the sand of the sea, and saw a beast rise up out of the sea, having seven heads and ten horns, and upon the horns ten crowns, and upon heads the name of blasphemy." In this case the 'sea' refers to the sea of humanity. The sand refers to the great population of the earth. Not only do these seven heads refer to Satan and his helpers, in another verse it's also described as the whole earth, meaning the seven continents.

Satan's war against God is explained in Chapter 10. It describes seven thunders who tried to entice Apostle John to include their message in Revelation. A 'voice from Heaven' told John not to write those things. It also describes a 'little book' Satan held in his hand that was 'sweet in the mouth but bitter in the belly.' Most certainly this is the little book Satan (not Gabriel) presented to Muhammad in the Cave of Hira near Mecca; which became the source of Islam. But, what significance is that seventh angel to our current times?

Verse 7 in Chapter 10 explains, "But in the days of the voice of the seventh angel, when he shall begin to sound, the mystery of God should be finished." Perhaps this mystery is beginning to be understood by revealing those other six angels of today. I have searched for these six stars, angels, for several years, and only now have I discovered a possibility of their identity. Verse 14 in Chapter 22 expresses blessings and salvation for those 'that do his commandments - that they may enter through the gates into the city.'

Verse 15 then describes the six evils that will not be allowed in, "For without are dogs, and sorcerers, and whoremongers, and murderers, and idolaters, and whosoever loveth and maketh a lie." Are these the six evil stars that accompanied Satan to earth when he was removed from Heaven? Can you take these evils that make their voices heard and apply them to many large groups that exist today? Hasn't that seventh angel begun to sound?

<h1 style="text-align:center">Article 25</h1>

<h1 style="text-align:center">Traitors and the Trojan Horse</h1>

Does this description sound familiar to the actions of the Democrats and the mainstream media to destroy our nation from within? It happened to Rome, that great empire that lasted a thousand years.

"A nation can survive its fools, and even the ambitious. But it cannot survive treason from within. An enemy at the gates is less formidable, for he is known and carries his banner openly. But the traitor moves amongst those within the gate freely, his sly whispers rustling through all the alleys, heard in the very halls of government itself. For the traitor appears not a traitor; he speaks in accents familiar to his victims, and he wears their face and their arguments, he appeals to the baseness that lies deep in the hearts of all men. He rots the soul of a nation, he works secretly and unknown in the night to undermine the pillars of the city, he infects the body politic so that it can no longer resist. A murderer is less to fear. The traitor is the plague." *Marcus Tullius Cicero, 58 B.C. Speech in the Roman Senate.*

The doors have been swung wide open by those inside our nation to invite those outside our nation to come in and destroy us. This happened to that great city Troy. Citizens of Troy were safe until they opened the gates and brought in their destruction. Troy was the perfect example of the importance of having a wall. Never forget the

Trojan Horse.

Article 26

The Purpose for Elected National Leaders

While I was pondering the question of the primary purpose for our national government I decided to ask that question online. This was the first definition that came up:

"The role of any national government is to protect the safety and well-being of its citizens and the sovereignty of the country's borders. National government is authorized to act based on a legal constitution, federal laws and accepted civil standards. All citizens benefit from agencies and programs created by national government."

Using this description as a simple guide then it becomes very clear, crystal clear, that elected Democrat officials are not fulfilling their primary role of government for the 'safety and well-being of its CITIZENS.' They are inviting and assisting many foreigners into our nation to destroy us, our moral character, and our manifest destiny as a God-loving nation. Furthermore, their actions and words now benefit non-citizens who disrespect our borders and our sovereignty. Their actions and words are aimed at making the CITIZENS of our great nation less respected and less protected. This is total abandonment of their primary purpose for being there; the safety and well-being of our CITIZENS. They are not just useless, they present a great danger to our survival as a nation.

Article 27
Drugs, Trumpets, and Beasts

Many have the feeling and understand that our nation and world is getting closer to that 'Great Crisis' period prophesied in Revelation. I was again touched by that feeling as I watched a program on TV called 'Border Wars.' It revealed that over a million pounds of drugs are seized at the checkpoints from Mexico each year; and at one location more that a thousand trucks pass through each day. One must wonder how many more millions of pounds of drugs flow into our nation. I also heard on a regular news program that more than a hundred people in the US die from drug abuse each day.

In my recent post I cited that Chapter 9 in Revelation identified the armaments and participants in that great war that's prophesied to come. The chapter before that, Chapter 8, explains one of the last events to occur before that happens. This announcement is made by the third angel of the seven angels with trumpets. All the other angels, with their trumpets, sound war related events.

The trumpet in verse 10 announced a great star called Wormwood falling to earth, "burning as it were a lamp, and it fell upon the third part of the rivers, and upon the fountains of waters." Verse 11 continues, "and many men died of the waters, because they were made bitter." Throughout Revelation, 'waters' refer to humanity; therefore the 'fountains of waters' must refer to the youth of our society. Obviously, that lamp refers to bongs or other things that make drugs stronger.

This trumpet is a great sign of things to come in the 'near' future, but there are others. One pertains to the number of beasts who will support Satan's war against God. Chapter 13 announces only two of these 'beasts' will appear. The first, Muhammad, died in 632 AD. In my opinion through much research is that Barack Obama, who claims to be a Christian (two horns of a lamb) but praises Muhammad, is the second beast. These are the only two beasts revealed in Chapter 13. There is no third beast on the horizon. Therefore......?

Throughout Revelation, 'waters' refer to humanity; therefore the 'fountains of waters' must refer to the youth of our society. Obviously, that lamp refers to bongs or other things that make drugs stronger. Wormwood is a wild plant that represents drugs. It's also the source of 'bitter' absinthe. Wormwood has already fallen. The next two trumpets presented in Chapters 8 and 9 introduce the beginning of that anticipated warfare. Does Wormwood suggest that time is near?

Now there are rockets and other missiles being exchanged on the border of Israel; and the activity seems to be increasing. But Revelation does not mention rockets; or does it? Let's examine Chapter 16, verse 21 for that answer:

"And there fell upon men a great hail out of heaven, every stone about the weight of a talent; and men blasphemed God because of the plague of this hail; for the plague thereof was exceeding great."

Since the words 'rockets and missiles' did not exist during John's time he used the word 'hail' to describe a similarity. At that time the weight of a talent was about 75 pounds or even somewhat heavier. At this very moment those 'hail stones' are being fired across Israel's border.

Perhaps these are two warnings to suggest a time is near to react as detailed in Matthew, Chapter 24, beginning with verse 15; to prepare and be ready. Could that 'Dome of the Rock,' the Islamic shrine that stands on the holy place, the Temple Mount, be that abomination of desolation 'spoken of by Daniel?' Stay tuned to those events at Israel's border.

Article 28
Five Democrat Goals

From Their Words and Actions These are Five Goals of Democrats to Destroy Freedom in America:

1. To redistribute wealth in our nation until all citizens have nothing.

2. To replace God with a powerful few to whom we must worship to survive.

3. To replace hope and aspirations with darkness and despair.

4. To make those who are now successful become subservient slaves.

5. To become leaders in the One-World Order; a power to destroy God's world.

Added: To destroy Donald Trump, the one who would protect our citizens, our Constitution, and our nation; perhaps even the world.

Article 29
Where are the Peaceful Muslims?

Many among us see Muslims as peaceful Muslims and radical Muslims. Is there a difference; can they be considered as separate and different? The answer to this question is absolutely not. Every Muslim on earth who is a real Muslim has the one goal of replacing Jesus with Muhammad, and with winning Satan's war against the real God of Heaven. This is made perfectly clear with only a few verses in Revelation, Chapter 17.

Chapter 17 begins with an angel inviting Apostle John to understand the great whore 'that sitteth upon many waters with whom the kings of the earth have committed fornication, and the inhabitants of the earth have been made drunk with the wine of her fornication.' This whore, this woman, this religion sits upon a scarlet colored beast, full of names of blasphemy, having seven heads and ten horns. This scarlet colored beast is the red dragon, Satan. Satan is the seventh angel in Chapter 10 who has sworn to remove God's time in Heaven. The other six angels came down from Heaven to help this seventh angel.

This woman is the totality of the Islamic religion. Verses 5-6 then give specific information about this woman. "And upon her forehead was a name written, Mystery, Babylon the Great, the Mother of Harlots and Abominations of the Earth. And I saw the woman drunken with the blood of the saints and with the blood of the martyrs of Jesus."

This reveals that Islam is the mother of those harlots and abominations; those terrorists and radicals. As revealed above, the 'woman' is drunken with the blood of the saints and with the blood of the martyrs of Jesus. This means that without the mother there could be no radicals. The mother is as guilty of terror against the world as are her harlots and abominations. There are no peaceful Muslims. They all plan the destruction of all that is not Islam.

Article 30

Hot nor Cold

Do you recall the statement from the Bible, 'You are neither hot nor cold?' This statement is taken from Apostle John's caution to the Christians at the ancient church at Laodicea, one of the seven churches of Revelation. This is a physical geological analogy John made to tell them they (and Christians today) should firm their obedience to the Word of God. This was taken from Revelation, Chapter 3, verses 15-16:

"I know thy works, that thou art neither cold nor hot: I would thou wert cold or hot. So then because thou art lukewarm, and neither cold nor hot, I will spue thee out of my mouth." So what is the analogy for these words?

The ruins of the church of Laodicea are in a rich plain below a small mountain several miles away. The ruins of the ancient city of Heiropolis are also near that rise. The name of the new small city is Denizli. At the very top of the mountain is an ancient Roman resort and spa named Pamukale. It has many hot springs that form calcium travertine pools. It's so brilliant and large that it's common name is 'Cotton Fortress.' So what does this have to do with 'hot nor cold?' When the running hot water reaches the fertile plain of Laodicea it's only lukewarm, neither hot nor cold.

During our visit there in 1974 we were allowed to play in the warm pools just like the old Romans did. Since the calcium and travertine began to wear and erode, no one is now allowed to get near the individual pools. To see beautiful scenes of that area visit Pamukale Photos online.

Article 31

Obama's Ring

How did my great interest in Revelation begin? Three events kicked me into high gear. First was after I read some and wondered about the reign of the 'beast's' seven heads. As I was on my morning walk I stopped in mid stride as I realized the beast's reign was not from the seven hills of Rome, but from the seven continents of the earth. Verse 9 in Chapter 17 confirmed this,

"The seven heads are seven mountains, on which the woman sitteth."
The 'woman' refers to the Islamic religion.

My interest peaked even higher when Obama was reelected even after giving greater praise to Islam than to America or Christianity. Chapter 13, verse 11 pointed another finger directly toward Obama as being one of the beasts in Revelation. "And I beheld another beast coming up out of the earth, and he had two horns like a lamb, and he spake as a dragon." In other words, he claimed to be a Christian but he supported only Islam; which Obama did with maximum intensity.

The third incident to heighten my interest pertained to Obama's ring. This is part of an article from 2012 that got my attention: "From Tea Party News - Inscription on Obama's ring. The Shahada is the first of the Five Pillars of Islam, expressing the two fundamental beliefs that make a person a Muslim: There is no god but Allah, and Muhammad is Allah's prophet. Sincere recitation of the Shahada is the sole requirement for becoming a Muslim." The engraving on his ring was of a serpent, not of the Shahada. This immediately reminded me of my visit to the ancient city of Pergamum, in Turkey.

Chapter 2, verse 13 describes Pergamos (Pergamum) as 'where Satan's seat is.' This seat of Satan is represented by serpents adorning the ruins of the Aesclepion a mysterious healing center there. The serpents on Obama's ring and these serpents of the Aesclepion reminded me of the same satanic source. After that my research into Revelation accelerated. Then many more clues and revelations evolved.

Article 32
An Invitation to Destroy Us

There are two specific Bible references that describe the approach that should be taken against those who plan to do us harm; individually, as a religion, and as a nation and world. This describes that 'religion of peace.' I avoid the name because some of my posts are being filtered. But everyone of pure heart knows who they are.

The first reference is from Second John, which has only 13 verses. All the verses are important, but verses 9-11 are very clear: "Whosoever transgresseth, and abideth not in the doctrine of Christ, hath not God. He that abideth in the doctrine of Christ, he hath both the Father and the Son. If there come any unto you, and bring not this doctrine, receive him not into your house, neither bid him God speed. For he that biddeth him God speed is partaker of his evil deeds." That evil 'religion' does not recognize Christ as the Son of God.

The second reference which is in Revelation describes exactly who they are. Chapter 17, verse 5 identifies this religion (woman) as Babylon the Great. Verse 6 points the finger directly to this religion, "And I saw the woman drunken with the blood of the saints and with the blood of the martyrs of Jesus."

This is our caution to anyone who seeks the Truth. Beware of those who invite them in to destroy us. Even Apostle John was deceived by her (verse 6) and "wondered with great admiration."

Article 33
May God Open Their Eyes

Although Democrats are doing everything they can to destroy Donald Trump and to increase the number of illegal aliens coming into our nation what will these same people do when their traitorous scheme backfires? Of course they and their cohorts, the mainstream media, will point their guilty fingers at Donald Trump.

It's documented that thousands more Muslims are infiltrating our borders along with South Americans. On 9-11 Muslims slaughtered 3000 of our innocent citizens. Democrats were patriots for a short pause after that horror, now they ignore these facts to destroy Donald Trump; and our nation.

It's Written in Revelation that devout Muslims (Harlots of Islam: Babylon the Great) will continue their blood lust against the world. Chapter 17, verse 6 reveals that they are 'drunken with the blood of the saints and with the blood of the martyrs of Jesus.' They have no reason to cease that blood lust against all that is good; they must sacrifice for their god Satan.

As a guilty young child answers when questioned about a mishap, the Democrats and their cohorts will answer, 'I didn't do it; it wasn't me. It was Donald Trump.' Just listen carefully to Democrats when another great disaster happens against America or the world. May God open the eyes of those who hate Donald Trump so much that they support and promote horror in the world.

Article 34
The Greatest Threat

Yesterday I read a post that Muslims were peaceful and only the terrorists (specifically ISIS) were the trouble-makers to be feared. Muslims promote themselves as 'peaceful' and have many convinced that's true. The great problem against this idea, however, is that wherever Islam exists there is no peace for anyone; only death and horror for those who are not Muslim. Their image and claim of peace is their ingrown tool to destroy other nations and religions; and people of good will toward others. How can a religion that worships Satan and is a tool of Satan to war against God in Heaven be a religion of peace?

The Bible describes Islam very clearly, and in many places. Perhaps the most basic and fundamental description of this image of peace versus terror in one religion is given in Revelation, Chapter 17, verses 5-6. This describes Islam as 'Mystery, Babylon the Great, the Mother of Harlots and Abominations of the Earth.' This is the mother religion. Then her spawn, those harlots and abominations, fulfill her mission in verse 6, "And I saw the woman drunken with the blood of the saints and with the blood of the martyrs of Jesus; and when I saw her I wondered with great admiration"

In this case, the author John was also amazed with the image of this woman; the one who spawned those terrorists and others who continue Satan's war against God. The 'mother' and her harlots will not be satisfied until they have fulfilled Satan's sworn oath described in Chapter 10.

In the past my posts have been rather lengthy and oriented toward both Islam and politics. Since I believe great troubling times are ahead I will focus my posts, perhaps with few exceptions, only on the increasing threat of Islam against the United States and the world. The Democrats are a great threat against our freedom, but perhaps not as great a threat as Islam is against the whole world.

Article 35
Source of the Koran

How did the Koran exist before Muhammad's Revelation? Who wrote it?

Have you ever wondered why Islam claims to be one of the three Abrahamic religions? There are two sources for this false claim. One source is from those who came after Muhammad. They claim they are descended from Ishmael, one of Abraham's sons. Even Muhammad denied this claim, since his documented ancestors were all from Arabia.

Islam's other claim of worshiping the same Christian and Jewish God comes from Muhammad's claim of being approached by an angel while he was contemplating in the Cave of Hira near Mecca. This explanation of the event is from Wikipedia (Muhammad and the cave of Hira:)

"Muhammad's revelation was an event described in Islam as taking place in 610 AD, during which the Islamic prophet, Muhammad was visited by the archangel Jibril, who revealed to him the beginnings of what would later become the Quran. The event took place in a cave called Hira, located on the mountain Jabal an-Nour, near Mecca.

According to biographies of Muhammad, while on retreat in a mountain cave near Mecca (the cave of Hira), Gabriel appears before him and commands him to recite the first lines of chapter 96 of the Quran. Muhammad's experience is mentioned in Surah 53:4–9." (Six lines of quote are then listed for Muhammad to recite. The article continues:

"Perplexed by this new experience, Muhammad made his way to home where he was consoled by his wife Khadijah, who also took him to her Ebionite cousin Waraqah ibn Nawfal. Waraqah was familiar with Jewish and Christian scriptures. Islamic tradition holds that Waraqah, upon hearing the description, testified to Muhammad's prophethood, and convinced Muhammad that the revelation was from God. Waraqah said: "O my nephew! What did you see?" When Muhammad told him what had happened to him, Waraqah replied: "This is Namus (meaning Gabriel) that Allah sent to Moses."

So, in summary the angel who visited Muhammad never said who he was; and where did the angel get that book (the Quran) from which he commanded Muhammad to recite? Chapter 10 in Revelation answers these questions.

Chapter 10 describes a mighty angel coming down from Heaven. That angel was Satan, not Gabriel. This was the seventh angel of the 'seven thunders' making their loud voices heard. Apostle John was told not to write what they uttered. These are Satan and his six angels who were removed from Heaven by Michael and his angels. As Satan held a little book in his hand he raised his hands to Heaven and swore to remove God's time in Heaven. When John 'ate the little book' it was sweet in his mouth but bitter in his belly. According to all the words and descriptions this little book can be none other than the formation of that little Islamic book that was presented to Muhammad in the Cave of Hira.

Verse 7 leaves a great prophesy of what's taking place today from that seventh angel, Satan, and his Islamic worshipers, "But in the days of the voice of the seventh angel, when he shall begin to sound, the mystery of God should be fulfilled."

Additional source information:

Before the revelation
Main article: Muhammad

"Muhammad was born and raised in Mecca. When he was nearly 40, he used to spend many hours alone in prayer and speculating over the aspects of creation. He was concerned with the "ignorance of divine guidance" (Jahiliyyah), social unrest, injustice, widespread discrimination (particularly against women), fighting among tribes and abuse of tribal authorities prevalent in pre-Islamic Arabia. The moral degeneration of his fellow people, and his own quest for a true religion further lent fuel to this, with the result that he now began to withdraw periodically to a cave named Mount Hira, three miles north of Mecca, for contemplation and reflection. Islamic tradition holds that Muhammad during this period began to have dreams replete with spiritual significance which were fulfilled according to their true import; and this was the commencement of his divine revelation.

The first revelation
The entrance to the Hira cave.

According to mainstream Islamic tradition, during one such occasion while he was in contemplation, the angel Gabriel appeared before him in the year 610 AD and said, "Read", upon which he replied, "I am unable to read". Thereupon the angel caught hold of him and embraced him heavily. This happened two more times after which the angel commanded Muhammad to recite the following verses:

"Proclaim! (or read!) in the name of your Lord who created:
Created man from a clinging substance:
Recite, and your Lord is the most Generous,–
Who taught by the pen–
Taught man that which he knew not."[Quran 96:1–5]

After the revelation

Perplexed by this new experience, Muhammad made his way to home where he was consoled by his wife Khadijah, who also took him to her Ebionite cousin Waraqah ibn Nawfal. Waraqah was familiar with Jewish and Christian scriptures. Islamic tradition holds that Waraqah, upon hearing the description, testified to Muhammad's prophethood, and convinced Muhammad that the revelation was from God.

Waraqah said: "O my nephew! What did you see?" When Muhammad told him what had happened to him, Waraqah replied: "This is Namus (meaning Gabriel) that Allah sent to Moses. I wish I were younger. I wish I could live up to the time when your people would turn you out." Muhammad asked: "Will they drive me out?" Waraqah answered in the affirmative and said: "Anyone who came with something similar to what you have brought was treated with hostility; and if I should be alive until that day, then I would support you strongly." A few days later Waraqah died.

The initial revelation was followed by a pause and a second encounter with Gabriel when Muhammad heard a voice from the sky and saw the same angel "sitting between the sky and the earth" and the revelations resumed with the first verses of chapter 74.

At-Tabari and Ibn Hisham reported that Muhammad left the cave of Hira after being surprised by the revelation, but later on, returned to the cave and continued his solitude, though subsequently he returned to Mecca. Tabari and Ibn Ishaq write that Muhammad told Zubayr:

"when I was midway on the mountain, I heard a voice from heaven saying "O Muhammad! you are the apostle of Allah and I am Gabriel." I raised my head towards heaven to see who was speaking, and Gabriel in the form of a man with feet astride the horizon, saying, "O Muhammad! you are the apostle of Allah and I am Gabriel." I stood gazing at him moving neither forward nor backward, then I began to turn my face away from him, but towards whatever region of the sky I looked, I saw him as before."

There is doubt about the period of time between Muhammad's first and second experiences of revelation. Ibn Ishaq writes that three years elapsed from the time that Muhammad received the first revelation until he started to preach publicly. Bukhari takes chapter 74 as the second revelation however chapter 68 has strong claims to be the second revelation." End of Wikipedia reference.

Article 36
Islam and the Pagan Moon God

From billionbibles(dot)org:

"Is Allah the God of the Bible, or is Allah the moon god of ancient Arabia?

Allah Moon God: While "Allah" could refer to God literally, the Allah of Islam is the moon god of ancient pagan Arabia.

The Arabic word for "god" is "ilah," while "al" is the Arabic for "the." Therefore, "Allah" combines "al" with "ilah" and removes the "i" to literally means, "the god." But much like "YHWH/Yahweh/Jehovah" is the personal name of the God of the Bible, "Allah" is also the personal name of the moon god, the chief among the three-hundred sixty pagan idols that were worshipped in Mecca, the home town of Muhammad. (Note: Muhammad destroyed all the worshiped idols except the moon god when he conquered Mecca.)

Is there evidence that Islam's "Allah" is the pagan moon god of ancient Mecca? Consider what the ancient pagan Arabians did to worship their moon god, Allah: they prayed while bowing toward K'abah, the "house of Allah" in Mecca that houses a meteorite - a rock from space - several times a day, visited it once a year, and walked around it several times during their visit.

To worship their Allah today: Muslims pray bowing toward the K'abah in Mecca five times a day. About two million Muslims visit Mecca every year and walk around the K'abah (the black cube, which is 40 feet tall). The Muslim "holy" month of Ramadan starts at the sighting of a new crescent moon.

Perched atop churches across the world is the cross, the symbol of the sacrifice made by the God of the Bible (see The Gospel). Perched atop mosques across the world is the crescent moon, the symbol of Allah whom Muhammad chose as the god of Islam." End of reference.

This pagan religion was captured by Satan when he visited Muhammad in the Cave of Hira near Mecca. The angel who visited Muhammad there was later claimed to be Gabriel, but the angel never said his name. Association with what that angel demanded of Muhammad and the 'little book' in Revelation, Chapter 10, clearly identifies the guiding document of Islam that was written to aid Satan's attack against God.

Article 37
Revelation's Plea to Hold Fast

As many Christians are aware, Christ and those who follow the Words are being attacked more violently every day. Some of those attacks are direct and violent while others are more insidious with soft "peaceful" persuasions. That prophesy of the final days is being fulfilled; that attack against God as defined in Chapter 10 of Revelation is becoming more defined. However, for those who seek salvation through the Truth, Christ left us clear and definite Words of understanding. In Chapter 2, verse 23 he cautions, "But that which ye have already, hold fast till I come."

The first Words of clarity are of time and events. Chapter 12 provides those clues by defining the meaning of 'time, and times, and half a time.' John, the author of Revelation, was aware that Jesus was in Egypt for three and a half years (Verse 6, 'a thousand two hundred and threescore days.) when His family escaped from King Herod. John used this analogy to describe two events of the future.

First was Constantine's adoption and protection of Christianity approximately 350 years later. (Verse 14, 'protected by two wings of a great eagle.' An eagle was the symbol of Rome.) After another 350 years (time and times and half a time) Christianity was no longer protected by Rome and came under a more vicious attack when Muhammad began the creation of Islam. This was approximately 700 AD. Verse 17 adds that 'The dragon (Satan-Islam) was wroth with the woman (Christianity) and went to make war against the remnant of her seed (today's Christians.) These events are also documented historically. Then Chapter 13 identifies two specific 'beasts' who will war against God (Christians and Jews.)

Chapter 13 begins by introducing a beast with seven heads. This beast is Satan and his six angels who were removed from Heaven by Michael and his angels. These were the 'seven thunders' mentioned in Chapter 10. Verse 3 in Chapter 13 introduces the first specific beast having a 'deadly head wound' that was healed. This describes Muhammad's wound at the Battle of Uhud in 624 AD. His troops thought he was dead and left the battlefield. They were surprised ('wondered') when he joined them in retreat. Verse 5 reveals 'power was given unto him to continue forty and two months.' Muhammad was poisoned in 628 and died in 632, forty two months later.

One of my recent articles describes my belief of the identity of that 'second beast' described in verses 11-18 as being Barack Obama. 'He had two horns like a lamb, and he spake as a dragon.' In other words he claims to be a Christian, but his words support only Satan's army, Islam. Verse 18 adds a final clue, 'count the number of the beast for it is the number of a man; and his number is Six hundred threescore an six - 666. The only way to count 666 is to add 6+6+6 which totals 18. So let's count: BARACKHUSSEINOBAMA. Isn't it also interesting that this information is confirmed by being presented in VERSE 18.

Article 38
How Deep is Their Hate?

I had another article planned for today pertaining to the beginning of the tribulation period, but I was distracted with one I just read about a millstone. This reminded me of something in Revelation about a great millstone. This great millstone is also about the time of tribulation. It's fully described in Chapter 18 and details the destruction of Islam, that Babylon in Revelation.

Babylon is one of the two religions (women) presented in Revelation. The other is Christianity. Christianity is introduced with the first two verses of Chapter 12. Islam is introduced in verses 5-6 of Chapter 17. Verse 6 states, "And I saw the woman drunken with the blood of the saints, and with the blood of the martyrs of Jesus."

Then Chapter 18 describes the complete destruction of Islam by a greater force. Verse 20 then says that Christianity will be avenged against this evil which has challenged God in Chapter 10. Chapter 18, verse 21 then explains the final blow against that Babylon the Great:

"And a mighty angel took up a stone like a great millstone, and cast it into the sea (sea of Islam humanity) saying, Thus with violence shall that great city Babylon be thrown down, and shall be found no more at all."

Verse 24 concludes with a repeat of that identity of Islam, described as Babylon the Great, "And in her was found the blood of the prophets, and of the saints, and of all that were slain upon the earth."

Since I believe, through reconciling other information in Daniel, Matthew, and Revelation, that this war might happen very soon I have a question about those who detest the foundation of our great nation. Will the Democrats and other American-haters support our nation and Donald Trump if we must go to war, as indicated, to defend our nation, our world, and our God? How deep is their hate against all that is Good?

Article 39
Their Plan to Destroy Us

Is Islam trying to infiltrate the United States by deception and from hiding? Why are so many of our national leaders and policy-makers allowing and supporting this infiltration of those who plan to come into our great nation to destroy our heritage and our freedom? It seems that those who are supporting this infiltration to destroy us are themselves part of the traitorous conspiracy. The Muslims are doing exactly what they have written and published that they would do to destroy our national identity. Their total plan, which is now in full attack, is written for all to see. The information at this link explains exactly what they are doing. Why are so many once loyal Americans now allowing and supporting thisr plan to destroy us?

After you click on this link then click on 'view the full document.' The document is in Arabic and English. The English version begins on page 16. You will be amazed.

A copy of this plan will also be included in the attachment at the end of this writing.

Article 40

Socialism is a Self-Destructive Objective

There's a motivation theory that explains the results between free Capitalism and controlling Socialism. It also explains much of the difference between management results and management failure. It's the Hierarchy of Needs Theory developed by psychologist Abraham Maslow in the early 1960s. It explains the progressive development from just existing to greatly succeeding. The basic model has five steps of needs in a hierarchy. These needs, according to the theory, are the things that motivate people to do something.

The basic need is the physiological need for food, water, warmth, and rest. Once these needs are fulfilled the next level is the safety needs. These include security and safety. Once these are fulfilled the next level of motivators is the belonging and love needs. This includes friends and personal relationships. The next higher motivator then becomes the need for esteem, which would include prestige and a feeling of accomplishment. The highest motivator then becomes the self-actualization needs such as creative activities and achieving one's full potential. An aware manager or leader recognizes this hierarchy and tries to allow each subordinate to recognize and fulfill his or her individual needs.

This concept applies not only to workplaces and other environments that need those involved to perform at their highest ability, it also applies to any environment or any nation. For a nation to succeed to its highest and most productive it must have people who have aspirations of personal fulfillment. This cannot be accomplished in a Socialist environment where people are promised a fair share for merely doing what they are assigned to do. This leaves them no ladder to climb.

That's why Socialism always fails. It doesn't allow or encourage anyone to reach the levels of esteem and self-actualization. The concept of fair share within Socialism is an assignment for personal failure.

I taught this concept at management seminars in the Memphis area in the early 1990s. The book I wrote and used for those seminars is still available at online sites. The title is, Managing Without Conflict: How to Create Extraordinary Productivity by Eliminating Ordinary Conflict.

Article 41

That Mark of the Beast

Today many believe that 'mark of the beast' mentioned in Revelation suggests a microchip will be placed in everyone's head or right hand in order to buy and sell in the world, and to perform other insidious monitoring of individuals. Since our world is rushing toward greater technology today that's not such a far out concept. However rest assured, especially the beautiful women, that a microchip will not be imbedded into your forehead to destroy your natural beauty. This is the verse in Revelation, Chapter 13, verses 16-17, that makes that prophesy referring to the beast:

"And he causeth all, both small and great, rich and poor, free and bond, to receive a mark in their right hand, or in their foreheads: And that no man might buy or sell, save he that had the mark, or the name of the beast, or the number of his name."

This mark in the foreheads simply means the acceptance of the beast Islam. This is reinforced in the next Chapter, 14, beginning with the first verse, "having his Father's name written in their foreheads." The 'mark in their right hand' simply means those who support Islam, including warfare and other murders of infidels. In many Muslim areas infidels are not allowed to participate in certain commercial activities. No ladies, your beautiful foreheads will not be disturbed.

Article 42

A Fair Share

Two pine trees, Loblolly and Longleaf, stood near a major road. Surrounding them below were lush green grasses which fed the wandering cows that provided milk; and blackberry and huckleberry bushes which gave delight to children roaming the area.

The two trees didn't look down to see what was beneath them. Instead they marveled at the rich beautiful leaves adorning the big oak tree across the road. Its canopy covered a large barren circle at its base.

One day Loblolly said, "Just look at that great, rich oak tree across the road. He has all those big bright leaves and keeps dropping those seed all over the place. All we have are skinny needles and a few seed in our cones, until some sneaky squirrel steals them then we have nothing." Longleaf added, "Yes, it's not right that we didn't get our fair share."

Later, a forest fire swept through and destroyed all the trees. Suddenly Loblolly and Longleaf found themselves as visions in the air and they saw Oaky's presence near them. Loblolly asked, "What happened?" Oaky answered, "It was our time; we served our purpose."

"But you were so rich and beautiful," Longleaf replied, "and you created so many seed that scattered everywhere to grow and grace the land."

Oaky said, "But you nurtured the earth with love and care. You helped others flourish so they might benefit from those seed I shared. You had more than a fair share."

Loblolly sighed, "Perhaps we all were blessed with a fair share. Perhaps we just express it in different ways to support a wonderful purpose."

Article 43
"Babylon is Fallen, is Fallen"

Are we nearing that time of tribulation revealed in the Books of Daniel, Matthew and Revelation? I can't answer this question definitively, but I have researched many signs that suggest those hardships are not far away. Of course, our distance from the flash point, the Middle East, will protect us somewhat, but here in America we will still have many uncomfortable times during the event. This clue is given in Revelation, Chapter 18, by the mention of ships on the sea and the profits from ocean trade. These verses refer to that great event:

Verse 2 states that "Babylon the great is fallen, is fallen, and is become the habitation of devils, and the hold of every foul spirit, and a cage of every unclean and hateful bird." Babylon the great is defined in Chapter 17 as the woman (religion) Islam. Verse 3 continues, "For all nations have drunk of the wine of the wrath of her fornication, and the kings of the earth have committed fornication with her, and the merchants of the earth are waxed rich through the abundance of her delicacies." (Unfortunately, even the Pope has welcomed Islam into his realm.)

Verse 9 continues, revealing that the earth shall lament for her (Babylon) 'when they shall see the smoke of her burning.' Verses 10-11 continue, "Standing afar off for the fear of her torment, saying, alas, alas that great city Babylon, that mighty city! For in one hour is thy judgment come. And the merchants of the earth shall weep and mourn over her; for no man buyeth their merchandise any more."

So here in the United States what will be a great sign that the Great War is beginning? It seems this sign will be when nations around Israel begin a major attack. And, even now Hamas, Syria, and Iran are assembling that horrible army for that attack. This includes the recent longer range missile tests by Iran. For what other reason would Iran (ancient Persia) want greater missiles?

Article 44
Those Who Hate President Trump

In my recent article titled, 'Why Have Walls?' I included these verses from Second Timothy, Chapter 3:

"This know also, that in the last days perilous times shall come. For men shall be lovers of their own selves, covetous, boasters, proud, blasphemers, disobedient to parents, unthankful, unholy, without natural affection, trucebreakers, false accusers, incontinent, fierce, despisers of those that are good, traitors, heady, highminded, lovers of pleasures more than lovers of God; Having a form of godliness, but denying the power thereof: from such turn away."

As we read these verses it's easy to recognize their meaning in total, but often we are too hurried to consider each individual condition for its deeper meaning. Each condition suggests its own meaning, but let's consider only two as clear examples of current events. The first that stands out to me is 'blasphemers.'

The first blatant examples that come to mind are Nancy Pelosi's comments; and the idea that newly-elected Muslims are accepted into a body that represents American citizens. Nancy Pelosi has used God's name to justify very late term abortions and refuses to help build a wall to protect us; American citizens who represent God's people. The new Muslims in our Congress claim to be of God, but they conform to the highest form of blasphemy; they place Muhammad on an order higher than Jesus.

The other is 'despisers of those that are good,' which would include 'false accusers.' Are there any of the 'heady' Democrats who do not openly, blatantly, and falsely accuse Donald Trump of horrible things just to show their deep hate? Those who most viciously call for President Trump's impeachment never express why he should be impeached. Is that not an act of covetousness?

Article 45
Golden Cup of Condemnation

Chapters 2-3 in Revelation give a great warning about a false prophetess who will lead many away from Christ. In his letter to the Church at Thyatira Apostle John writes that the name of this false prophetess is Jezebel; but this is simply an analogy of the real seducer who entices many away from Christianity. This is a timely prophesy; exactly what's happening today. In that letter, he wrote:

"I have a few things against thee, because thou sufferest that woman Jezebel, which calleth herself a prophetess, to teach and to seduce my servants to commit fornication and to eat things sacrificed unto idols. Behold, I will cast her into a bed, and them that commit adultery with her into great tribulation, unless they repent of their deeds."

This prophesy is made timely, for events today, from further identification explained in Chapter 17. It defines the modern Jezebel which that analogy represented.

Chapter 17 then gives another description of that whore Jezebel 'that sitteth upon many waters, With whom the kings of the earth have committed fornication, and the inhabitants of the earth have been made drunk with the wine of her fornication. Having a golden cup in her hand full of abominations and filthiness of her fornication.' This is her golden cup of peaceful enticement.

Then verse 5 describes this whore Jezebel, "And upon her forehead was a name written, Mystery, Babylon the Great, the Mother of Harlots and Abominations of the Earth." Verse 6 explains exactly who she is, "And I saw the woman drunken with the blood of the saints and with the blood of the martyrs of Jesus." Verse 6 adds, "And when I saw her I wondered with great admiration."

Only one woman (religion) fits these descriptions; Islam. Islam claims to be based on a prophet, a false prophet, and they eat things sacrificed unto an idol; a black stone in Mecca. As Apostle John 'wondered with great admiration when he saw her,' so does even the Pope, today, admire and accept that religion as being equal with Christianity. God help those who don't understand and are enticed into this Jezebel's golden cup of condemnation.

Article 46
Voters Beguiled by that Sweet Book

Many today are asking how so many declared Muslims are getting elected to high political offices. Other than Democrats voting from the graves and other unauthorized places, the answer is given very clearly in the Book of Revelation. This includes deception by our recent president who claimed to be a Christian, but supported only Islam; which is also described in Chapter 13 of Revelation.

This support for declared Muslims is explained in two Chapters of Revelation. Chapter 10 describes a 'little book' Satan held in his hand. In verse 10 John wrote, "And I took the little book out of the angel's hand, and ate it up; and it was in my mouth sweet as honey; and as soon as I had eaten it, my belly was bitter." In other words, Islam offers words of sweetness and peace, but the results are bitterness and horror. This little book is the one offered to Muhammad in the Cave of Hira by Satan; not Gabriel as they claim. That angel never revealed who he was.

In Chapter 17 even Apostle John was beguiled by Islam 600 years before that woman (religion) appeared. Verse 5 reveals Islam as 'Babylon the Great, the mother of harlots and abominations of the earth.' Verse 6 continues, "And I saw the woman drunken with the blood of the saints and with the blood of the martyrs of Jesus." Then John added that he was beguiled by her, "and when I saw her, I wondered with great admiration." Although John saw her, described her, and knew of her deadliness, he was still amazed by Islam's presence.

Islam continues, for fourteen centuries, to wreak horror against humanity claiming to be 'sweet' yet they behead innocent men, women, and children for no reason of humanity; simply at the whim of some dislike. Too many in our world continue to be beguiled by that 'sweet little book' as even John was 'wondered' by her presence. Those who vote for them are beguiled to support Satan.

Article 47

When Will Babylon attack Israel?

As many of you suspect, or know, I do research daily trying to interpret more Words and verses in Revelation. I think I have already written that there's no question about the identity of Islam in Revelation. That's given in Chapter 17:

Verse 5 identifies a woman (religion) as Mystery, Babylon the Great, the Mother of Harlots and Abominations of the Earth. Verse 6 gives her clear identity, "And I saw the woman drunken with the blood of the saints and with the blood of the martyrs of Jesus." There is no other religion on earth except Islam that gets a drunken high by killing Christians or anyone else who is not Islam. That slaughter is carried out by the zealous harlots and terrorists killing on behalf of that mother Babylon who hides behind that cloak of 'peace.'

But when will that great attack, that final showdown between Good and Evil happen? No one knows 'the day nor the hour' but there's information in Thessalonians that gives a general clue for those who believe. It's somewhat lengthy but please read and be patient. It begins in Chapter 5, verse 2:

"For yourselves know perfectly that the day of the Lord so cometh as a thief in the night. 3) For when they shall say, Peace and safety; then sudden destruction cometh upon them, as travail upon a woman with child; and they shall not escape. 4) But ye, brethren, are not in darkness, that that day should overtake you as a thief. 5) Ye are all the children of light and the children of the day: we are not of the night, nor of darkness. 6) Therefore let us not sleep, as do others; but let us watch and be sober."

In conclusion, those of us who worship God are of the light and are not asleep as to what's happening is our world today. We see that evil that's dominating the Middle East waiting for the perfect moment to attack Israel; as the conversation in the world gets more focused on 'peace and safety.' Those of the light are watching from the Words. Those who do not believe are wandering in the darkness and will be shocked when that 'thief in the night' arrives to destroy Israel.

Additional referenced Information:

Iran and Israel Closer Than Ever to All-Out War – Iran Fires Missiles Into Israel, Israel Responds With Guided Missile Launch, by Michael Snyder | Jan 22, 2019 | FEATURED ARTICLES, MIDDLE EAST, POLITICAL, SUPPORT ISRAEL, TERRORISM, U.S. NEWS, WATCHMEN ON THE WALL, WORLD NEWS:

"Israel and Iran are edging dangerously close to a state of all-out war.

On Sunday night, Israeli forces rained missiles down on Iranian forces based in the Damascus area "for nearly an hour". According to the IDF, this was a response to "dozens" of missiles that were fired by Iranian forces in Syria toward targets in Israel earlier that day. The Israelis were able to intercept the Iranian missiles, but if any of them had gotten through they could have caused a tremendous amount of damage. Some of the missiles that Israel fired at the Iranians were reportedly intercepted, but quite a few of them did hit their intended targets. If the violence continues to escalate, we could potentially soon be talking about an all-out war between Israel and Iran in which both sides use their weapons of mass destruction.

The missile strikes against Iranian targets in Damascus made headlines all over the globe. According to Syrian state media, there were "consecutive waves of guided missiles."

Syrian state media cited a Syrian military source as saying Israel launched an "intense attack through consecutive waves of guided missiles", but that Syrian air defenses destroyed most of the "hostile targets."

Witnesses in Damascus said loud explosions rang out in the night sky for nearly an hour.

The Syrians are boasting that they were able to destroy quite a few of the Israeli missiles, but independent observers confirm that quite a few Iranian targets were destroyed.

In the past, the Israelis have not always publicly acknowledged their attacks in Syria, but on Sunday night they released an immediate statement…

"We have started striking Iranian Quds targets in Syrian territory," Israel's military said in a statement.

"We warn the Syrian Armed Forces against attempting to harm Israeli forces or territory."

You can see some footage of the missile strikes right here. Among the targets were "weapons warehouses at the Damascus International Airport"…

Targets striked by the IDF, which number at around 10 according to its statement, include weapons warehouses at the Damascus International Airport and in other locations, an Iranian intelligence site and an Iranian training camp in Syria's south.

Now that the Iranians have been hit so hard, will they respond by striking back at Israel?

If both sides continue to escalate the violence, eventually a "point of no return" will be reached, and then all hell will break loose.

Prior to the IDF missile attacks on Iranian targets, rockets were fired toward the Golan Heights from inside Syria, and Israel blamed those attacks on the Iranians…

The Israeli military said earlier on Sunday that missiles fired toward the northern Golan Heights were intercepted by the Iron Dome missile defense system. It added in a statement on Monday that an

Iranian force fired these missiles, but said it holds the Syrian regime responsible for any activity in its territory.

It seems extremely unlikely that this conflict will be resolved any time soon. The Iranians are certainly not going to leave Syria, and they are definitely going to continue to funnel arms and resources to Hezbollah forces in southern Lebanon.

And the Israelis have clearly stated that they are going to resist any Iranian attempts to strengthen Hezbollah or to establish a permanent military presence inside Syria. In fact, Israeli Prime Minister Benjamin Netanyahu couldn't have been any clearer when he said this to reporters…

"We have a permanent policy, to strike at the Iranian entrenchment in Syria and hurt whoever tries to hurt us," Israeli Prime Minister Benjamin Netanyahu said.

If a full-blown war erupts in the days ahead, Israel will almost certainly find itself fighting Iran, Syria and Hezbollah simultaneously. Of course Hezbollah is essentially an Iranian proxy, and at this point they have between 130,000 and 150,000 missiles aimed at Israel. When war finally comes, it will be extremely bloody and extremely destructive.

Tonight, we are closer to such a war than ever. The Iranians and the Israelis absolutely hate one another, and now they are firing missiles at one another.

It isn't going to take much to push the two sides over the edge, and if that happens we are just a hop, a skip and a jump away from the start of World War 3.

About the author: Michael Snyder is a nationally-syndicated writer, media personality and political activist. He is the author of four books including Get Prepared Now, The Beginning Of The End and Living A Life That Really Matters. His articles are originally published on The Economic Collapse Blog, End Of The American Dream and The Most Important News. From there, his articles are republished on dozens of other prominent websites. If you would like to republish his articles, please feel free to do so. The more people that see this information the better, and we need to wake more people up while there is still time. Republished with permission The Most Important News. End of reference.

Article 48

Where Are They?

They Must Come Forward and 'Talk About That.'

In another article I asked the question; why don't our Christian leaders and teachers speak about the dangers and horrors to come as explained in the book of Revelation. I believe there are two reasons for their reluctance to teach us of that urgent message in Revelation.

First is the intense pressure that would be put upon them by our current outspoken anti-Christian and anti-God society. That predominant social pressure is to demean and degrade anyone who speaks the truth about God and religion. Many of our elected leaders and other influential speakers will not tolerate Christian truth; especially that Christian truth pertaining to the blatant attack against God and reasonable humanity by Satan and his growing army. Perhaps our Christian leaders are apprehensive of the pressure they would have to endure if they come forward with the Truth of Revelation and the full outspoken Word of God.

Second, perhaps those who should be our spiritual and salvation leaders are hesitant to come forward to give us the true Words of meaning because they have misinterpreted the words of warning from Revelation itself. Perhaps verses 18 and 19 in Chapter 22 are the basis for their withdrawal:

"If any man shall add unto these things, God shall add unto him the plagues that are written in this book: And if any man shall take away from the words of the book of this prophesy, God shall take away his part out of the book of life and out of the holy city, and from the things which are written in this book."

Perhaps many church leaders interpret this to mean giving their interpretations of this prophesy. However, it means exactly what it says: add to or take from. It does not mean to interpret in faith. This is explained in Chapter 1, verse 3:

"Blessed is he that readeth, and they that 'hear' the words of this prophecy, and keep those things which are written therein, for the time is at hand." In addition, at the end of each of the seven letters to the seven churches in Asia (the whole world even today) is written,

"He that hath an ear, let him 'hear' what the Spirit saith unto the churches."

The conclusion; if anyone is to hear, then is it not reasonable to expect that someone in authority and with knowledge should explain to those who cannot read or have access to the written Word? Those Christian leaders and teachers must come forward to present the message in Revelation to God's people; to encourage them to 'Hold fast.'

What gave me the clue for this article? I recently spoke to a friend who is a retired pastor about Revelation. His very quick answer was, "We can't talk about that." But they must come forward and 'talk about that.'

Article 49
Stench Still Rises

I found this very interesting. If I had not seen the reference at the end of this quote I would have sworn it referred to Barack Obama and most of his cabinet members and advisors such as Brennan, Clapper, Hillary, Eric Holder, Loretta Lynch, Susan Rice and Samantha Power while Obama was in office. His stench was so great it even soaked into the hearts and souls of most current Democrat leaders who touched his hand while he was in office. Obama still leads a negative influence on America even after he left those visible halls of government. This is that quote:

"A nation can survive its fools, and even the ambitious. But it cannot survive treason from within. An enemy at the gates is less formidable, for he is known and carries his banner openly. But the traitor moves amongst those within the gate freely, his sly whispers rustling through all the alleys, heard in the very halls of government itself. For the traitor appears not a traitor; he speaks in accents familiar to his victims, and he wears their face and their arguments, he appeals to the baseness that lies deep in the hearts of all men. He rots the soul of a nation, he works secretly and unknown in the night to undermine the pillars of the city, he infects the body politic so that it can no longer resist. A murderer is less to fear. The traitor is the plague." *Marcus Tullius Cicero, 58 B.C. Speech in the Roman Senate*

Article 50
Assaults on America

America, the greatest country that's ever existed to recognize and protect humanity and to encourage freedom and opportunity, is now in grave danger to maintain those wonderful gifts for mankind. Our wonderful nation is now under attack by fierce zealots who can't tolerate the ideas, opportunities, and freedom of aspirations America allows and supports. We are now on a dangerous precipice.

One of these three assaults is from direct confrontation by radical Islamic Jihadists who proclaim, promise, and boast they will destroy us and our way of life; especially our Christian way of life. Their whole being is to control the world and they don't keep their intentions or their goals secret. It's a blatant military and terrorist attack. America is the 'Great Satan' they must destroy to fulfill their religious and zealous mission.

The other two assaults are not direct or open. They are subtle and insidious, and are guided by deception. And, presently no one is combating their insidious and sneaky encroachment on our accepted American way of life. The leaders and encroachers have been free to spout their evil and their harmful designs without resistance.

One encroachment is from the Muslim Brotherhood. They even have a written plan to replace American freedoms with their dogmatic religion through a process they call 'Settlement.' With the support of Barack Obama and others within our government they are far advanced in accomplishing that plan.

The other assault is from a socialist-communist agenda outlined by Saul Alinsky; and is being accomplished through his 'Rules for Radicals' program. Barack Obama was once a teacher of the Alinsky principles. In her early years, Hillary Clinton also corresponded with Alinsky and praised his radical programs.

To further explain this relationship and following among Alinsky, Obama, and Hillary Clinton, this is an article titled 'Obama, Hillary Clinton, Saul Alinsky and Rules For Radicals.' It was written from his diary by Donald Ayotte on January 13th, 2012 and posted on redstate.com:

"Saul Alinsky's book. "Rules For Radicals," was first named "Rules For Revolution," and has caused untold controversy since Alinsky published the book in 1971. I realize that one diary will not be enough to communicate the content of destruction this book holds for our Republic.

When I first bought the book, I vowed to read it cover to cover before donning my pencil to write even one word. Alinsky opens in the book's prologue by writing, "The revolutionary force today has two targets, moral as well as material. Its young protagonists are one moment reminiscent of the idealistic early Christians, yet they also urge violence and cry, "Burn the system down!"

Alinsky's tactics were based not on Stalin's revolutionary violence, but instead on the neo-Marxist strategies of Antonio Gramsci, an Italian communist. Relying on gradualism, infiltration and the, "dialectic process" rather than bloody revolution. Gramsci's transformational Marxism was so subtle that few even noticed the deliberate changes.

At this point, I would like to define, "dialectic process:" Reasoning in which question-answer approach (dialectic) is used to examine the correctness, legitimacy, or validity of an assumption, idea, opinion.

Alinsky writes on page 10, "A Marxist begins with his prime truth that all evils are caused by the exploitation of the proletariat by the capitalists. From this he logically proceeds to the revolution to end capitalism, then into a new social order, or the "dictatorship" of the proletariat and finally the last stage, the political paradise of communism."

A letter from Saul Alinsky's son David States: "Obama learned his lesson well. I am proud to see that my father's model for organizing is being applied successfully beyond local community organizing to affect the democratic campaign in 2008. It is a fine tribute to Saul Alinsky as we his approach 100th birthday."

Obama taught workshops on Alinsky's theories and methods for years and in 1985, he started working as a community organizer for and Alinskyite group called, "Developing Community Projects." While building coalitions of black churches in Chicago, Obama was criticized for not attending church and decided to become an instant Christian. He then helped fund the Alinsky Academy. Obama was a paid director of the Woods Fund, which is a non-profit organization used to provide start-up funding and operating capital for Midwest Academy, which teaches the Alinsky tactics of community organization. Obama sat on the Woods Fund Board with William Ayers, the founder of the, "Weather Underground," a domestic terrorist organization.

Hillary Rodham as a student at Wellesly in 1969, interviewed Saul Alinsky and wrote her thesis on Alinsky's theories and methods. She concludes her thesis by writing, "Alinsky is regarded by many as the proponent of a dangerous socio/political philosophy. As such he has been feared, just as Eugene Debs or Walt Whitman or Martin Luther King has been feared, because each embraced the most radical of political faiths, "democracy."

Alinsky offered Hillary a job upon graduation from Wellesley but she decided to attend Yale Law School where she met her husband Bill Clinton.

"Rules For Radicals," page 113, "From the moment the organizer enters a community he lives, dreams, eats, breaths, sleeps only one thing and that is to build the mass power base of what he calls the army. Until he has developed that mass power base, he confronts no issues."

Page 59, "But to the organizer, compromise is a key and beautiful word. It is always present in the pragmatics of operation. It is making a deal, getting that vital breather, usually the victory. If you start with nothing, demand 100 percent, compromise for 30 percent, you're 30 percent ahead."

In closing, I would urge every conservative or constitution minded person to know your enemy. Buy and read this book. Your adversaries have memorized it and are using the principles within its covers to destroy our great republic. Make no mistake, the Progressive Liberals or Radicals' goal is to tear down the republic and shred the Constitution. The problem is, they have nothing to replace it with; they are only bent on destruction.

A Nation can only be disgraced by the failure of its citizenry to take action in the face of tyranny. Donald Raleigh Ayotte August 2010." End of reference.

Three terms are identified in this message of change. One is 'Useful Idiots.' The others are 'Useful Innocents' and 'Useful Fools.' Although the three terms were not specifically described and defined, perhaps they should be considered. From an observation in this modern day, 2015, and the political activities that are now taking place, they will be easy to define:

Useful Idiots

A useful idiot is an activist who follows a leader and echoes that leader's ideologies and terminology to influence others to blindly follow in that desperate path to destroy something, not to make it better. The tactic of the leader and the useful idiots who promote and support him or her is simply to destroy a status quo with a declaration that the status quo is bad - and things will improve after it's totally destroyed. There is no definition of that which is to 'be better.' One doesn't have to be a politician to be a useful idiot. Many expose themselves in 'letters to the editor' and other such blogs and editorials; often making harsh personal attacks on those with whom they disagree. Their attacks are always personal on the person.

Useful Innocents

Useful innocents have not been fully described or defined. However, after much research on the subject, the definition of a useful innocent has become perfectly clear. A useful innocent is a 'prole' as described in George Orwell's book '1984.' This is the definition which follows the definition of the 'Low' in his book: one who is concerned only about existing at home, does just enough work without expectation or preparation for more success, hopes things will get better when new leaders are selected, and votes for new leadership that promises to make life better - he never questions the person or the source of the promises.

Useful Fools

Useful fools are not defined at all at any source. Therefore, let me submit one for consideration. A useful fool is one who detests the status quo and is never satisfied with anything. He or she wants change just for change sake. And when there is change, he or she is never satisfied with that. The Constitution, honor, truth, and loyalty are unknown and irrational concepts. The only thing that matters to the useful fool is that something be 'changed.' Could this be the reason for Obama's great focus on 'Change' during his first campaign for president?

Obama and his close association of Useful Idiots condemn 'millionaires and billionaires' as cheating and not helping the poor and middle class. How much of their millions would they part with to help you? If you asked either of them for a dollar or a hundred dollars, do you think they would give it to you? Are there any examples, whatsoever, where they have given part of their millions to help anyone - only one single individual? Yet, their useful idiots guiding their legions of useful innocents follow their every word as if it were meant for their personal financial salvation.

If all the money in the United States were equally divided, every person would be poor. No one would have enough money to build businesses and create jobs. In that case, should those brave and bold people who risked their money to start a small business that might grow into a large business be penalized to keep everyone equal. If that were the case, then there would be only a destitute and bleak future for the United States. That's what Obama and Hillary Clinton are suggesting we have in America. And, what's worse is that their 'Useful Idiots' fully support them without even one question of the outcome.

Article 51
Satan Attacks Donald Trump

I usually spend my Bible research in those areas related to Revelation; such as Daniel, Chapters 9 and 12 and Matthew, Chapter 24. I was flipping pages just now and came across two verses in Matthew that focused hard my attention. Both verses are in Chapter 11, in which Jesus is addressing some Pharisees.

First is verse 25: "Every kingdom divided against itself is brought to desolation; and every city or house divided against itself shall not stand."

Next is verse 29: "Or else how can one enter into a strong man's house, and spoil his goods, except he first bind the strong man? And then he will spoil his house."

After I considered for awhile I realized this is the perfect explanation of why Democrats and other extremists against the purity of our great nation are trying so hard to bind and destroy the 'strong' man of our house. It's so they can 'spoil' our house and replace it with Socialism or Islam, those satanic beasts.

This association is so clear it cannot be misinterpreted. They must bind and destroy the leadership of Donald Trump so they will have free reign to destroy our God-given house, the United States of America. At this time of our history, who else is in a position to replace him who has the purity of heart to acknowledge the strength and Words of Christ?

God bless America.

Article 52
Great Collusion!

The special investigation against Donald Trump for 'collusion' started over two years ago. Any reasonable and sane person knew even at that time that it was a made-up charge to destroy our president. The great charge by Democrats and the mainstream media at that time was 'collusion' even though that's not even considered a crime. If it were a crime it would be labeled 'conspiracy.' I believe a conspiracy was and is being committed but not by Donald Trump. That 'bombshell' hit me this morning.

The guiding word for a long time was 'collusion.' That word finally decreased by the Democrats and the mainstream media. A few days ago the guiding word was 'manufactured crises.' This morning when I began listening to the news the new catch word is 'bombshell!'

Now let's return to 'reasonable and sane person.' Any reasonable and sane person would clearly understand that when all the catch words change at the same time that's not just collusion; it's a conspiracy. There's no doubt that someone is leading a great conspiracy, which is a crime, to destroy our president and our great nation. Many of the Democrats and much of the media are part of this designed conspiracy. Who is at the top organizing and leading that great conspiracy?

Is it a major Democrat, or is it one of their Russian friends with whom they are committing collusion?

Article 53

Islam's Great Deception and Acceptance

I just read an article giving details of the growing number of deaths from Islamic extremism throughout the world. The article is: Islamist extremism caused 84,000 deaths worldwide in 2017, by Olivia Gazis, September 13, 2018 / 6:24 PM / CBS News. This is a summary:

"A new report tracking the roots, spread and effects of violent Islamist extremism found that 121 groups that share elements from a common ideology are now operating worldwide. Their activities resulted in the deaths of 84,000 people – nearly 22,000 of them civilians – in 66 countries in 2017, the report found. In remarks at the Council on Foreign Relations in Washington, DC, former British Prime Minister Tony Blair said on Thursday that Islamist extremism is "global and growing."

This should be no surprise to anyone. Revelation clearly identifies these terrorists and the action they will wreak upon the earth. Chapter 13, verses 5-6 identifies Islam as "Mystery, Babylon the Great, the Mother of Harlots and Abominations of the Earth. And I saw the woman drunken with the blood of the saints and with the blood of the martyrs of Jesus." Her harlots are these terrorists ravaging the earth. Chapter 18, verse 24 adds, "And in her was found the blood of prophets, and of saints, and of all that were slain upon the earth." (Islam is that mother, that 'common ideology,' identified in the article.)

One example of abominations is their treatment of young children as their sex slaves. The world accepts this abominable act as their 'religion.'

Apostle John gave an example of Islam's acceptable horror against humanity by his observation at the end of verse 6 above, "And when I saw her, I wondered with great admiration." This explains why so many support Islam's incursion to destroy a civil society. They are awed by their fear and wonder. This is his warning of the great deception of Islam who claims to worship God; but instead, worships Satan.

Article 54
The Destroyer

God 'wanted Donald Trump to become president,' Sarah Sanders says.

In an interview on Wednesday with Christian Broadcasting Network White House press secretary Sarah Sanders said she believes that God wanted Donald Trump to be president.

"I think God calls all of us to fill different roles at different times and I think that He wanted Donald Trump to become president," Sanders said, according to CBN News. "That's why he's there and I think he has done a tremendous job in supporting a lot of the things that people of faith really care about."

Many of us who looked at the alternative during the last election believed it was a miracle that Donald Trump was elected. We knew the alternative would have been a disaster for America and the world. At 2:00 in the morning when those 5 votes came in from Pennsylvania I closed my eyes and thanked God for protecting America once again. Later, while still researching for answers in Revelation I finally understood that great event.

My research and analysis is that the major war in the Middle East is coming very soon that will emerge into world-wide consequences. Syria, Iran, and Hamas are already building up their forces, rockets and missiles preparing for that attack.

Chapter 9 in Revelation gives details of the armaments and personnel who will be involved with that warfare. The first verse states that a star from Heaven will be given the key of the bottomless pit, not to the bottomless pit. This represents knowledge and determination of one who represents God's forces that will defeat Satan's forces of Islam. The 'bottomless pit' is a synonym of warfare. Then verse 11 explains who this king, this selected angel, is:

"And they had a king over them, which is the angel of the bottomless pit, whose name in the Hebrew tongue is Abaddon, but in the Greek tongue hath his name Apollyon." Research suggests this name refers to 'destruction' or 'destroyer.' Now, who could be this destroyer? An article by newrepublic gives the answer. It begins, 'Trump Is Not a

Builder. He's a Destroyer.' Below is a link to that article. Is there any question now as to if and why God choose Donald Trump to have that key of the bottomless pit?

https://newrepublic.com/article/143074/trump-not-builder-hes-dest royer

Article 55
Is the Message Clear?

One of my articles asked the question; does Revelation really reveal. More of my recent articles have focused on interpreting codes that reveal times and events to understand that the time of horrors is approaching us gradually and cautiously, 'like a thief in the night.' But when those times of horror begin how will we know what to expect that will indicate the beginning of those difficult times? The 'four horses of the apocalypse' introduced in Chapter 6 give the general overview; an introduction of those things to come.

The first horse, the white horse, 'went forth conquering, and to conquer.' This reveals God's conquest over those represented by the second horse, the red horse.

The red horse: 'and power was given to him that sat thereon to take peace from the earth, and that they should kill one another; and there was given unto him a great sword.' This represents the two parts of Islam that traditionally 'kill one another' as they ride as one to 'take peace from the earth.' Also, Islam began with a sword and the sword is still used today to behead many not favored by Islam.

The third beast introduced the black horse with a rider that had 'a pair of balances in his hand' as a voice said, 'A measure of wheat for a penny, and three measures of barley for a penny.' This represents a great trade disaster across the world, especially the shipment and availability of food. Most trade by sea will be halted when warfare begins in the Middle East. Great starvation will occur. This is explained in Chapter 18 which lists the devastation of many merchants. It begins with the demise of Babylon the great, Islam, in verse 2:

"And he (the angel) cried mightily with a strong voice, saying, Babylon the great is fallen, is fallen." Verse 3 adds, "and the kings of the earth have committed fornication with her, and the merchants of the earth are waxed rich through the abundance of her delicacies." Verse 11, "And the merchants of the earth shall weep and mourn over her; for no man buyeth their merchandise any more." Then the next verses describe many of those things that will not be shipped by sea. Verses 17-18 conclude, "For in one hour so great riches is come to nought, and every shipmaster, and all the company in ships, and sailors, and as many as trade by sea, stood afar off, And cried when they saw the smoke of her burning, saying, What city is like unto this great city!"

Then verse 24 describes this great city, Babylon the great, only as Islam should be described, "And in her was found the blood of the prophets, and of saints, and of all that were slain upon the earth."

The fourth beast introduced the fourth horse, the pale horse, in Chapter 6, "And his name that sat on him was Death, and Hell followed with him. And power was given unto him to kill with sword, and with hunger, and with death, and with the beasts of the earth." These are deaths caused by people killing people, hunger, natural causes for lack of medicines, and by the beasts (insects and parasites of the earth.) These horrors could include a quarter of the earth's population.

Many things are now happening in the Middle East. Could this be that beginning?

Article 56

A Fair Share or a Job?

Other than morality and safety, what's the most important thing for an adult to have? The answer is a source of survival income. This ordinarily means a job. Although this is a simple and basic concept, it's an idea totally foreign to those who stand on the sidelines screaming for their FAIR SHARE because rich people have too much; they have more than they need! They are led to believe from scheming Democrats and Socialists that being rich is a great sin; and it must be reconciled with higher taxes. This is the promise that separates humanity and destroys societies. Those 'useful idiots' or other lazy people simply refuse to understand a fundamental of money.

Where do these 'useful innocents' think jobs come from? Jobs come from needs of people and from excess money rich people have to fulfill those needs. Farm workers wouldn't have jobs if people didn't need food and the land owner didn't have enough money to hire those workers. Clerks at grocery stores wouldn't have jobs if store owners didn't have enough money to build their stores. Houses wouldn't be built if rich people didn't have excess money to invest for loans to build those houses. The examples go on and on. Perhaps a perfect example is the one where 25,000 potential jobs were abandoned in New York because that Congresswoman didn't want Amazon to have more money.

For a nation and a society to survive there must be jobs; and there must be people with enough money to create those jobs. And, according to Money and Banking principles the income from one job has a turnover rate of seven times. For example, the paid store clerk uses that income to buy a product or service from someone else. This means that one job helps create income and support to seven other workers, until finally tax gets the remainder.

A job is also important in other ways. It gives the conscientious worker a source of pride and an example of service and community.

Article 57
What is a Fair Share

I just submitted this as a letter to the editor. Recently my letters have been 'too strong' and they have refused to publish them. Let's see if they publish this one:

One of the promises of rising socialism is for everyone to have a fair share. Since I'm not sure what a fair share is I searched for a definition. Merriam-Webster described it as 'a reasonable amount.' Therefore a fair share would be defined individually from one's point of view. Today there are two extreme points of view.

First would be the point of view from a Capitalist, a free-enterprise person. This view likely would be, 'It's reasonable that I have what I have because I worked hard, had a job as a teenager, tried to do my best in school, and never found an excuse not to be the best I could be at my job, whatever that job was. I was always focused to be successful. Therefore what I have is a reasonable amount for my success at reaching my target.'

Then there is the view from the other end of the extreme. 'I never had a chance to be successful and have enough money to survive as well as I would like. I waited and looked for jobs, but had to turn many down because they didn't pay enough. I never got a break like those rich people who have more than they need. That opportunity never came my way.'

It's very clear. Those who never see their goal for success will never get there. Something to be reached must first be defined. Perhaps a fair share is from the achievement of aspirations, not more free stuff.

Yes. It was accepted and published as a letter to the editor.

Article 58
The Fair Share Dagger

Beginning with Barack Obama, every Democrat who opens his or her mouth to spew words uses the term 'fair share' referring to what they promise their followers; those useful idiots who believe their deceptive promises. Since I wasn't sure what a fair share is I asked for the definition on google. Google gave me a definition from Merriam-Webster. That definition is 'a reasonable amount.'

So, one might ask if you have a 'reasonable amount' of money. That all depends doesn't it? First it would depend upon what one likes to do with money. Is it to just barely get by; to take a great vacation to Paris; to send children to college; or possibly to add rooms onto a house for a large and growing family?

The Democrats have used this deceptive dagger to weaken Republicans since Obama campaigned for President. Obama swooned over that concept and that promise. Possibly this was the subtle dagger that destroyed his Republican opponents. And, the Republican opposition never asked Democrats that simple and direct question: what is a fair share?

What the hell are Republicans afraid of? Why are they afraid to challenge that question and that vague concept of a fair share? If demagoging Democrats are asked that question directly and forcefully, they will never be able to give an answer that would support their position. Just Do It!

Article 59
Lenin, Stalin, and Elizabeth Warren

I watched a series on TV this morning titled: Stalin Apocalypse. The series covered much of Lenin and the Bolsheviks then Stalin and his Proletariat. After that I watched Elisabeth Warren's announcement as a candidate for President of the United States. All the speeches and announcements seemed to be from the same speech mold.

Lenin and the Bolsheviks claimed to be fighting against oppression and unfair tactics by the Czar and the upper class in Russia. They strengthened the unions and demanded a fair share of the wealth for everyone. Violence erupted against that upper class. Czar Nicolas and his family were murdered. Their guiding mantra was 'Peace, Land, and Bread.'

Stalin rose through the ranks of Lenin's Marxist organization and eventually gained control of the whole nation then absorbed other nearby nations creating the USSR. At that time Stalin didn't make many public speeches because he was a Georgian and spoke with a conspicuous Georgian accent. But he had many followers who spoke for him and increased his power hold by intimidation, deadly force and promises to the working class. His movement was called the Rise of the Proletariat, which meant the rise of the working class. Proletariat is the base word for the description of 'Proles' in George Orwell's book, '1984.' Later they were described as those 'useful idiots' and 'useful innocents.'

Useful Idiots were the targets of Warren's speech today. She promised the same thing Lenin and Stalin promised: fair share, destroying wealthy people by confiscating their excess wealth, strong unions to give working class more power, free education to give everyone an equal opportunity, and on, and on, and on. She promised everything Lenin and Stalin promised. But, as those Proles in Orwell's book found out; all they got was death and despair.

What those power hungry zealots ignore to express is that without enough rich people there will never be enough wealth to share for everyone; everyone who makes a determined effort to earn their fair share from those jobs and opportunities created by wealthy people.

It's so sad. It seems useful idiots will always be useful idiots. More to come with more Democrat (not Democratic) announcements.

Article 60

That Fear of Drowning at Birth

The Democrats' elation of approving near birth murder of babies not only made me sad, it also made me wonder and try to recall what I might have felt at birth. After much concentration I recalled many times having a dream of almost drowning, but I raised my head above water and took a fantastic deep breath of life that not only surprised me it also saved my dream life. I have heard many people who expressed they have had the same or similar dream. Finally I remembered, but that's the only thought at birth that I remember.

I was very comfortable then all of a sudden there was brightness and my chest began to tighten and restrict. There was that strong urge to bring something into my chest but I was afraid to allow my chest to accept that substance whatever it was. I was afraid of the pain that might result. I was aware of pending pain. Suddenly I gasped and was surprised that it was something that took away all my pain and apprehension. I didn't know at the time that it was my first gasp of air.

If you think of your past deep memories of that dream, or even the event itself, you might remember that great feeling of joy from the absence of pain when you took that first breath of something that you didn't know was called air and oxygen.

The Democrats are elated that they can now inflict that great pain upon those near-born persons. Yes, they know pain, but they don't know the word of 'pain.' But, since many Democrats refuse to accept the Grace of God, perhaps they also refuse to accept the idea of God protecting humanity by gracing all life with the fear of pain. All animals are innately born with that fear. God bless America, and protect those who can't protect themselves.

Article 61

That Thief in the Night

The Book of Revelation gives no direct information about a time that will begin the great battle between Babylon the Great (Islam) and Christ's forces. The only approximate time reference is when the third trumpet sounded and the great star Wormwood fell to earth, making the waters bitter and causing many to die (Chapter 8.) This wormwood represents the great drug epidemic which is taking place today causing many people to die. The next trumpets announce the actual warfare events. The great question of today is when will that fifth trumpet sound to announce the beginning of that great disaster. How near is it and how will we know? Perhaps a chapter in Daniel helps us find that answer.

Chapter 9, verse 26 reveals that "the people of the prince (prince with the minor p represents Satan) that shall come shall destroy the city and the sanctuary, and the end thereof shall be with a flood, and unto the end of the war desolations are determined." Then verse 27 suggests an approximate time:

"And he shall confirm the covenant with many for one week; and in the midst of the week he shall cause the sacrifice and the oblation to cease, and for the overspreading of abominations he shall make it desolate, even until the consummation, and that determined shall be poured upon the desolate."

Could this 'covenant with many for one week' be that nuclear agreement with Iran for seven years? That agreement was made in July, 2015; we are now in the 'midst' of that seven years. A covenant has never been made in the past with any nation to protect Israel; only this current nuclear agreement. Even in Obama's last year in office he allowed a vote by the world body not to protect Israel's unified lands. He refused to use that veto to protect Israel against those who wish to destroy that sacred land.

As many have read, that horror will begin as 'a thief in the night.' Iran is now very desperate due to the many sanctions. But what could they do blatantly to impair the United States that would allow them to attack Israel militarily, knowing that America is committed to protecting Israel? As 'a thief in the night' they might attack America's ability to respond quickly with many simultaneous cyber attacks. That might fulfill that prophesy 'as a thief in the night.' Are we prepared for that thief if he silently slithers into our realm of defense? Let's hope so; for if not it's written that Israel and the whole world will suffer great horror.

Article 62

Interesting Word Derivatives

I was researching some words the other day in Revelation and came across something I thought was very interesting. It's about the source and evolution of words. For example just one letter added to or taken from these two words explain their purpose.

For GOD, just adding another O results in GOOD.

For DEVIL, just removing the D results in EVIL.

Was it a coincidence or did someone in long ago history intentionally create these associative words for a purpose?

Article 63
Apollyon and Abaddon the Destroyer

Chapter 9 in Revelation sets the stage for the upcoming Battle of Armageddon. It explains an angel given a key of the bottomless pit to war against the one who challenges God's reign in Heaven. Most interpret this chapter as defining a horrible beast who will lead scorpions, locusts and other beasts to attack mankind. Verse 11 says that the king over them will be the angel of the bottomless, not from the bottomless pit, 'and his name will be Abaddon and Apollyon.' The real interpretation is that this Apollyon will lead Christ's forces on the battlefield to destroy Satan's army, Islam. Bottomless pit is an analogy for warfare.

In my research I discovered that the Abaddon and Apollyon names are ancient names referring to Destruction or Destroyer. With current events now taking place with battleships, rockets, and missiles being positioned in the Middle East, I suspect that Donald Trump would be the Abaddon or Apollyon leader of the forces that will destroy that great evil. My research confirms that Trump has already been given that title of Destroyer. This list of online articles points directly to that name:

Donald The Destroyer: Assessing The Trump-Effect thepolemicist .net/2017/07/donald-destroyer-assessing-trump-effect.html

Donald Trump: Destroyer In Chief - The Daily Banter dailybanter.com/2018/06/15/donald-trump-destroyer-in-chief

Trump the Destroyer by Lucy P. Marcus - Project Syndicateproject-syndicate.org/commentary/trump-devastation-div ersionary-tactics-by...

Donald the Destroyer: Assessing the Trump Effect counterpunch.org/2017/07/28/donald-the-destroyer-assessing-the-tr ump-effect

Donald Trump, destroyer of democracies - Chicago Tribune chicagotribune.com/opinion/letters/ct-letters-donald-trump-robert- mueller...

Taibbi on Trump the Destroyer – Rolling Stone rollingstone.com/politics/politics-features/trump-the-destroyer-127 808

Donald the Destroyer - counterpunch .org

Donald The Destroyer: It Only Took 2 Years To Crush ISIS reddit.com/r/The_Donald/comments/b43jy5/donald_the_destroyer_ it_only_to

More about the Destroyer:

In further research I learned that the Abaddon and Apollyon names are ancient names referring to Destruction or Destroyer. I also suspected that Donald Trump would be the leader of our great forces, not horrible monsters, to destroy Satan's army. But, why the title 'Destroyer.' More research just gave me that answer. It's from an article by Peter Sifre on July 3, 2018 as reported in newsbusters.org.

This is part of that article:

"On Tuesday's edition of New Day, hosts John Berman and Alisyn Camerota conducted a panel on President Trump's list of potential candidates for retiring Justice Kennedy's seat on the Supreme Court. During the segment, CNN political analyst Brian Karem made his animosity towards President Trump and the conservative movement quite clear. Apparently, conservatives make Karem "nauseous."

The panel began its discussion by examining Judge Brett Kavanaugh and his writings on executive privilege based off his work in Ken Starr's investigation of the Clinton Administration. Karem responded saying that Trump's consideration of Kavanaugh was "Trump the destroyer in action. I mean, this is the man who wants to tear down everything."

This suggests very strongly that if President Trump 'the destroyer' is to be the leader of that action, then that Great Battle might be just over the near horizon. Has Abaddon or Apollyon already been assigned? If this is so then what happens in the near future should not be a surprise.

Article 64

Protecting America

The role of any national government is to protect the safety and well-being of its citizens and the sovereignty of the country's borders. National government is authorized to act based on a legal constitution, federal laws and accepted civil standards. All citizens benefit from agencies and programs created by national government.

Obama's Best Contribution to America

What was Obama's best and only contribution to the benefit and security of our nation? Answer: his deceptive and insidious support and promotion of Islam, ISIS, and anarchy prompted millions of loyal citizens to rush to the gun stores to buy guns and ammunition. The demand was so great that many gun and sporting stores were sold out of popular guns and ammunition for months. Thank you Obama for creating that more defensive posture of our national patriots.

https://www.reference.com/government-politics/role-national-government-440663ca5040b051

Article 65
Obama's Mission

America's beginning wasn't easy or predestined. It took citizens of courage and wisdom not only to create that vision, but also to take those first bold steps. They sacrificed everything to give those who would come after them un-imagined freedom and opportunity. They saw only a future of prosperity, caring, decency, and fellowship for those later citizens.

The people's decision on November 6, 2012 changed that American dream their ancestors had fought so hard to fulfill. They elected Barack Hussein Obama as president of the United States of America. That was the day the bullet was intentionally and prophetically fired directly through America's heart. That's the day America began to lose its patriotic blood.

The election for his first term, 2008-2012, was a new American experiment, a risky experiment. A virtually unknown, untested, and inexperienced person was elected as president of the most powerful country on earth.

His known background and experience was only that of a community organizer. In that role his main goal was to teach people of low income and low aspirations how to get more things and benefits from the government without producing anything of worth in return. While hard-working and conscientious citizens were tasking themselves to benefit themselves, their families, and their great country, Barack Hussein Obama was teaching others how to take from their dedicated efforts without contributing anything in return. His first election was the day the hammer was cocked to fire that fatal bullet to destroy America.

Immediately, as president, his first actions were to divide Americans by class, income, race, ethnicity, and social status. He used a sharp carving knife to sever the nation, to exclude the successful with high aspirations from those who just wanted more free stuff; more of what he promised them, their 'fair share.'

His economic and social ideologies are directly opposite from President Kennedy's. Kennedy said, "Ask not what your country can do for you, ask what you can do for your country." Clearly Obama's ideology has been, "Ask not what you can do for your country, ask how much more free stuff you can get from your country." Since Obama's first inauguration our national debt has gone from four trillion dollars to sixteen trillion dollars. He is desperate to spend much more that American can afford. Why is he so intent on bankrupting America?

My writings give two possible answers. One is biblical and one is geopolitical. Is he positioning himself to be the leader of the coming New World Order? Or, has Satan selected him to be the leader of his army on Earth to destroy the Spirit of God? My current research and writings are in search of this answer.

Article 66
Revelation Really Reveals

There are many 'beasts' mentioned in Revelation, but only two are identified as real people. These are the first beast and the second beast introduced in Chapter 13. The other two specific beasts against God are Satan and Islam. Then there are the four beasts around the throne of God, in Chapter 4, who introduce the four horses of the apocalypse in Chapter 6 that will bring disasters upon the earth. It seems these beasts are the messengers of God who will see these events into the future as those horses go forth. Apostle John was given the visions and the Words to describe these two physical people, beasts, who appear many years after his prophesy.

Two entries in Chapter 13 identify Muhammad as that first beast, the Antichrist. Although there are many antichrists, there is only one 'the' antichrist as stated in 1 John, Chapter 2, verse 18. Chapter 13 reveals he had a deadly head wound that was healed, 'and all the world wondered after the beast.' Muhammad was wounded in the head at the Battle of Uhud in 625AD and fell as dead. His troops left the battle field believing he was dead, but later he miraculously joined them in retreat. (Online research: Battle of Uhud.) Verse 5 gives the second identity of Muhammad: 'and power was given unto him to continue forty and two months.' Muhammad was poisoned in 628AD and died in 632AD. He 'continued.' (Online research: wikiislam, The timeline of Muhammad.)

Verse 10 announces the death of that first beast, then verse 11 announces the arrival of another beast, that second beast the false prophet, with 'two horns like a lamb, and he spake as a dragon.' This clearly identifies Barack Obama, who claimed to be a Christian but spoke words of support only for Islam and that dragon, Satan. Verse 12 adds, "and he causeth the earth and them which dwell therein to worship the first beast, whose deadly wound was healed." The next verses describe his use of airpower 'wonders of making fire come down from the sky' to deceive men. In other words, his deception of claiming to fight ISIS allowed ISIS to grow and have more influence in the Middle East and even worldwide. This fulfilled the prophesy of verse 15 of giving power to that image of the beast ISIS that 'should both speak, and cause that as many as would not worship the image of the beast should be killed.'

Apostle John wrote these things hundreds and thousands of years before they happened; and his words were very specific with verified facts. How could he have known these things without the visions and Words given to him from God? How can anyone with any sense of reason at all suggest that God and his Son Christ are not real? Even now, as prophesied, there is a great war against God and Christians. But real Christians know how this war will end. Where are our Christian Church Leaders?

Article 67
More Real Revelations

It seems Christianity is being attacked from every corner of the world today, with both deeds and words. Christians are being slaughtered and slandered everywhere, and even more Democrats and Progressives are denying the Words of God more and more every day. Even pastors, priests and other church leaders seem reluctant to go beyond 'faith and goodness' sermons to warn their followers of real threats to their lives and to God's Words. By now most Christians already know how to 'worship God, believe in Jesus, and be kind to one another.'

I watched a science program on television yesterday that basically concluded that Jesus and Christianity was a myth created from the activity of a troublemaker about 2000 years ago. That program prompted this entry. This current threat to humanity is in clear detail in Apostle John's writing of Revelation. This is a real warning far beyond 'love thy neighbor.'

John was the last of the apostles. He spent years exiled on Patmos where he wrote Revelation, then was released at an old age to return to Ephesus where he died peacefully. There is even a monument to him in the ruins of Ephesus still today. When he wrote Revelation his writings reveal he had access to the writings of the other apostles, especially those of Matthew, since many of the phrases are similar; especially Chapter 24. But John's writings include more specific prophesy. In Revelation, John gave us an approximate time of specific events to come. Those times have clearly arrived. That prophesy is about the arrival of a beast, approximately 700 AD, whose purpose is to war against God and to kill those who worship God. This input will be only a short summary. With this summary however, one should be able to interpret more of Revelation.

A major clue is the interpretation of the words 'waters' and 'sea.' These generally refer to people and humanity, since our bodies are mostly water. Chapter 10 refers to the beginning of Satan's promise, his oath, to defeat God on earth and in Heaven. He holds a 'little book' that will be the guide for his army to war against God. Then Chapter 12 describes the arrival of Christ on earth and the immediate attack against Him by Herod; and the family flees to Egypt where He is protected for 'a thousand two hundred and threescore days.' This represents three and a half years which unlocks the code of 'time, times, and half a time' (1+2+1/2.)

Approximately 350 years later, Constantine reunited Rome (two wings of a great eagle) and protected Christianity for the next 350 years. That put the time at approximately 700 AD which was the beginning of Islam. According to Muslim history, while Muhammad was 'contemplating in the Cave of Hira, near Mecca, he was presented with a 'little book' from which to read. They later claimed this book was presented by Gabriel, but consider who was holding that little book in Revelation, Chapter 10.

The last verse in Chapter 12 gives the conclusion and the purpose for Islam; considering that there are two women described in Revelation. The first is Christianity. The other is the 'mother of harlots and abominations of the earth,' Islam, described in Chapter 17.
"And the dragon was wroth with the woman and went to make war with the remnant of her seed, which keep the commandments of God, and have the testimony of Jesus Christ." This is the war we are facing today, and it's Satan's sworn oath to increase this war and to win his battle against God. We must understand this to understand what's happening in our world today.

Article 68
Still A Great Danger to the World

An article titled 'Obama: America Not a Christian Nation' written by John Eidsmoe at thenewamerican usnews on 15 April 2009 reads: "President Barack Obama stated at a press conference in Turkey last week that we Americans do not consider ourselves a Christian nation, or a Muslim nation, but rather, a nation of citizens who are, uh, bound by a set of values."

Obama has made similar statements in the past. In June 2007, he told CBS, "Whatever we once were, we are no longer a Christian nation — at least, not just. We are also a Jewish nation, a Muslim nation, a Buddhist nation, and a Hindu nation, and a nation of nonbelievers."

Note the progression. In 2007, he said we are no longer "just" a Christian nation. Now, in 2009, he says we "do not consider ourselves a Christian nation" at all."

Another article from thetruthwins (,) com reveals twenty quotes from Obama supporting Islam:

#1 "The future must not belong to those who slander the Prophet of Islam"

#2 "The sweetest sound I know is the Muslim call to prayer"

#3 "We will convey our deep appreciation for the Islamic faith, which has done so much over the centuries to shape the world — including in my own country."

#4 "As a student of history, I also know civilization's debt to Islam."

#5 "Islam has a proud tradition of tolerance."

#6 "Islam has always been part of America"

#7 "we will encourage more Americans to study in Muslim communities"

#8 "These rituals remind us of the principles that we hold in common, and Islam's role in advancing justice, progress, tolerance, and the dignity of all human beings."

#9 "America and Islam are not exclusive and need not be in

competition. Instead, they overlap, and share common principles of justice and progress, tolerance and the dignity of all human beings."

#10 "I made clear that America is not – and never will be – at war with Islam."

#11 "Islam is not part of the problem in combating violent extremism – it is an important part of promoting peace."

#12 "So I have known Islam on three continents before coming to the region where it was first revealed"

#13 "In ancient times and in our times, Muslim communities have been at the forefront of innovation and education."

#14 "throughout history, Islam has demonstrated through words and deeds the possibilities of religious tolerance and racial equality."

#15 "Ramadan is a celebration of a faith known for great diversity and racial equality"

#16 "The Holy Koran tells us, 'O mankind! We have created you male and a female; and we have made you into nations and tribes so that you may know one another.'"

#17 "I look forward to hosting an Iftar dinner celebrating Ramadan here at the White House later this week, and wish you a blessed month."

#18 "We've seen those results in generations of Muslim immigrants

– farmers and factory workers, helping to lay the railroads and build our cities, the Muslim innovators who helped build some of our highest skyscrapers and who helped unlock the secrets of our universe."

#19 "That experience guides my conviction that partnership between America and Islam must be based on what Islam is, not what it isn't. And I consider it part of my responsibility as president of the United States to fight against negative stereotypes of Islam wherever they appear."

#20 "I also know that Islam has always been a part of America's story."

Obama has made over 20 statements praising and supporting Islam, yet he claims to be a Christian. His background has proven him to be a deceiver of the highest order. Perhaps his history and his actions have proven him to be that 'second beast' of Revelation described in Chapter 13, verses 11-18. It begins:

"And I beheld another beast coming up out of the earth (humanity); and he had two horns like a lamb, and he spake as a dragon." This means he claims to be a Christian but he speaks words favoring only Islam's god, Satan. The next few verses then explain how he uses deception to allow an image of the beast (ISIS representing the beast, Satan's Islam) to be alive and active to force people to become Muslims. Then we have that infamous 'mark of the beast' to consider.

Many believe that 'mark' of the beast is a computer chip or some other control device. Simply, this mark in the right hand represents someone actively enforcing Islam upon others. The mark in the forehead represents those who accept Islam in their minds. This is confirmed by words in the first verse in Chapter 14, whereby those who accept God have His name written in their foreheads. Now we come to that number 666 puzzle. Verses 17-18 say to count the number of the beast's name. The only way to count 666 is to add 6+6+6 which is 18. Therefore 18 letters reveal the name: BARACKHUSSEINOBAMA. Obviously, the pass code is identified by being written in VERSE 18.

According to Revelation, this second beast is still a great danger to Christianity and the whole world. And, Obama is still actively spreading his deception to defeat God's Word.

Article 69
More Codes in Revelation

My previous articles give several interpretations to help understand some of the coded clues in Revelation. I believe if more of these clues are interpreted and understood then more people seeking the Word of God would be more excited about reading Revelation. It's also vitally important that this prophecy be understood to know how to prepare for what's coming in the future; possibly the very near future.

The association of Chapter 8 with Chapter 9 is vitally important to understand an event and the time of that event. This clue is presented with the sounding of seven trumpets. The third trumpet announced a bitter 'great star' falling from Heaven burning as it were a lamp. The star was named Wormwood. Research of this name revealed wormwood is a wild plant grown in many places that produces drugs including the bitter substance which is the basis of absinthe. This clearly represents the great drug problem that exists across the world today. The star was 'burning as it were a lamp' reinforces the idea of drugs with the use of the lamp, a bong.

The fourth trumpet presents three 'woes' to follow. Then the fifth trumpet announced the first of the woes which was the activities of the 'bottomless pit.' The bottomless pit represents warfare. Chapter 9 gives descriptions to explain that warfare after a star from Heaven 'was given the key of the bottomless pit.' This was not the 'angel from the bottomless pit' as is often misinterpreted.

Verse 2 reveals that smoke came out of the bottomless pit when it was opened. Verse 3 adds, "And there came out of the smoke locusts upon the earth; and unto them was given power, as the scorpions of the earth have power.' Then more descriptions were given:

'The shapes of the locusts were like unto horses prepared unto battle; and on their heads were as it were crowns like gold, and their faces were as the faces of men. They had hair as the hair of women, And their teeth were as the teeth of lions. And they had breastplates as if of iron. And they had tails like unto scorpions.'

To many these wild descriptions are interpreted as some wild creatures of imagination; which discredits their acceptance of Revelation. But to anyone who has been in a major battle zone these identities are very clear and distinguishable. Locusts are simply squadrons of aircraft on the horizon. Scorpions are simply helicopters twisting about on a flight line. Teeth of tigers are the front grills of armored military combat vehicles. Faces of women are simply women from the cockpit of an aircraft. I observed most of these things while I was an Air Force officer on the flight line in Saigon in 1966. They are not horrible monsters rising from the earth.

The general time has been given to us. The horrors to come have been explained to us. Then; Chapter 9 in Daniel, Chapter 24 in Matthew, and Revelation have been given to us to know what to expect and when to expect it. I am preparing. Are you?

Article 70
Time Event Codes

Yes, Revelation really reveals. More of my recent articles have focused on interpreting codes that reveal times and events to understand that the time of horrors is approaching us gradually and cautiously, 'like a thief in the night.' But when those times of horror begin how will we know what to expect that will indicate the beginning of those difficult times? The 'four horses of the apocalypse' introduced in Chapter 6 give the general overview; an introduction of those things to come.

The first horse, the white horse, 'went forth conquering, and to conquer.' This reveals God's conquest over those represented by the second horse, the red horse.

The red horse: 'and power was given to him that sat thereon to take peace from the earth, and that they should kill one another; and there was given unto him a great sword.' This represents the two parts of Islam that traditionally 'kill one another' as they ride as one to 'take peace from the earth.' Also, Islam began with a sword and the sword is still used today to behead many not favored by Islam.

The third beast introduced the black horse with a rider that had a 'pair of balances in his hand' as a voice said, 'A measure of wheat for a penny, and three measures of barley for a penny.' This represents a great trade disaster across the world, especially the shipment and availability of food. Most trade by sea will be halted when warfare begins in the Middle East. Great starvation will occur. This is explained in Chapter 18 which explains the devastation of many merchants. It begins with the demise of Babylon the Great, Islam, in verse 2:

"And he (the angel) cried mightily with a strong voice, saying, Babylon the great is fallen, is fallen." Verse 3 adds, "and the kings of the earth have committed fornication with her, and the merchants of the earth are waxed rich through the abundance of her delicacies." Verse 11, "And the merchants of the earth shall weep and mourn over her; for no man buyeth their merchandise any more." Then the next verses describe all those things that will not be shipped by sea. Verses 17-18 conclude, "For in one hour so great riches is come to nought, and every shipmaster, and all the company in ships, and sailors, and as many as trade by sea, stood afar off, And cried when they saw the smoke of her burning, saying, What city is like unto this great city!"

Then verse 24 describes this great city, Babylon the Great, only as

Islam should be described, "And in her was found the blood of the prophets, and of saints, and of all that were slain upon the earth."

The fourth beast introduced the fourth horse, the pale horse, in Chapter 6, "And his name that sat on him was Death, and Hell followed with him. And power was given unto him to kill with sword, and with hunger, and with death, and with the beasts of the earth." These are deaths caused by people killing people, hunger, natural causes for lack of medicines, and by the beasts (insects and parasites of the earth.) These horrors could include a quarter of the earth's population.

Many things are now happening in the Middle East. Could this be that beginning?

Article 71
A Blessed Nation

Comments have been posted recently about the question; should we regard ourselves a Christian nation. Perhaps that question should be; are there enough Christians in our nation that God will continue to bless us. Perhaps a name for ourselves is less important than the foundation of our lives that represents the character of our nation.

I remember the years after WWII ended. Everyone knew we were a nation blessed by God; no one would have spoken any words against that acceptance. With His blessing America saved the world from the

Axis powers' satanic dreams, and confirmed freedom to the world. That feeling lasted many years until it filtered away in later generations. Later generations had not felt that wonderful blessing recovering from that world-wide horror, therefore they were not touched by that wonderful feeling. Now many are led from His blessings by 'false prophets and false apostles' as described in John's letters to the seven churches of Asia.

Perhaps we can imagine Barack Obama was referring to the demographic diversity of America when he proclaimed 'we are no longer a Christian nation' although we know exactly what he meant in his blatant support for Islam. Some might believe his proclamation was to weaken and denigrate the relationship between America and Christ; while others might consider his comment as merely a demographic observation.

Thanks to our president, Donald Trump, the recognition of Christ's blessings and influence on our nation has returned to our nation's house. That recognition flows out and encourages Americans who feel that blessing within our personal lives. Yes, the basic character of our nation is still that America is a Christian nation; although there are many demographics within.

Article 72
The Red Horse

The Red Horse and the Scarlet-Colored Beast are introduced in Revelation. The first mention is of the red horse and his rider in Chapter 6 as one of those four horses of the Apocalypse. He was introduced by the second beast described in Chapter 4, verse 7 as 'like a calf.' If you recall from my last article, the rider of the first horse, that white horse, 'went forth conquering and to conquer.' He was introduced by the first beast, 'like a lion.' His specific conquest according to these verses suggest is to slaughter that rider of the red horse as slaughtering a 'calf.'

Information about that rider of the red horse continues in Chapter 6, verse 4, "and power was given to him that sat thereon to take peace from th earth, and that they should kill one another; and there was given unto him a great sword." The next reference to this red (color) horse is in Chapter 12, verse 3, "And there appeared another wonder in heaven; and behold a great red dragon, having seven heads and ten horns, and seven crowns upon his head." Then verse 4 states that this dragon stood before Christianity 'ready to be delivered to devour her child (Jesus) as soon as it was born.' The purpose and goal of the rider on that red horse was to destroy Christianity, as reiterated further in verse 17:

"And the dragon was wroth with the woman, (Christianity) and went to make war with the remnant of her seed, which keep the commandments of God, and have the testimony of Christ." Then Chapter 17 explains the identity of the rider of this red horse and how they will 'kill one another.'

Chapter 17 begins with an angel coming forth to explain this rider, (verse 4; the woman) sitting upon a scarlet colored beast. Verses 5-6 then explain the two parts of this one rider. It's the mother religion, the woman, and her offspring, "And upon her forehead was a name written, MYSTERY, BABYLON THE GREAT, THE MOTHER OF HARLOTS AND ABOMINATIONS OF THE EARTH. And I saw the woman (the mother and the harlots combined) drunken with the blood of the saints and with the blood of the martyrs of Jesus." Only one religion - all parts of the religion - is excited and celebrates the slaughter of saints and those who follow Jesus. That Babylon the Great in totality is Islam. The mother celebrates when her offspring slaughter God's people. But how will this one rider 'kill one another?'

There are two parts of Islam; the Sunnis and the Shiites. The harlots and abominations of both are considered the whore. These are the offspring identified as 'radicals.' Verse 16 explains the conclusion, "And the ten horns which thou sawest upon the beast, these shall hate the whore, and shall make her desolate, and naked, and shall eat her flesh, and burn her with fire." Verse 17 adds, "For God hath put in their hearts to fulfil his will."

Since Christ 'went forth on the white horse to conquer' Chapter 19 explains that conclusion after that great battle. Verse 20 explains that the beast and the false prophet were 'cast alive into a lake of fire.' Verse 21 adds, "And the remnant were slain with the sword of him that sat upon the horse, which sword proceeded out of his mouth; and all the fowls were filled with their flesh." My previous article explained His twoedged sword.

Article 73
Beasts and Swords

A previous article mentioned four beasts around God's throne. This is described in Revelation, Chapter 4, verses 6-8. It tells of these four beasts as 'full of eyes before and behind.' Each also had six wings, 'and they were full of eyes within and they rest not day and night.' This means they could see everything in the past and in the future; and each of these beasts had a special task of prophesy as suggested by their individual descriptions in verse 7, "And the first beast was like a lion, and the second beast like a calf, and the third beast had a face as a man, and the fourth beast was like a flying eagle."

These four beasts made their appearance in Chapter 6 to detail events of the future as they announced the 'four horses of the apocalypse' that would bring the great war and the tribulation period. Each horse was released as the first four seals of the book were opened. These were the seals of the book described in Chapter 5 that only Christ could open.

The first beast 'like a lion' introduced the white horse upon which sat a rider who 'went forth conquering and to conquer.' Chapter 19, verses 11-21 give the details of Christ's conquering of those enemies. Verse 11 confirms who this rider of the white horse is, "And I saw heaven opened, and behold a white horse; and he that sat upon him was called Faithful and True, and in righteousness he doth judge and make war."

Two verses, 1:16 and 2:16, describe His weapons of war: "and out of his mouth went a sharp twoedged sword; Repent; or else I will come unto thee quickly; and will fight against them with the sword of my mouth." Then Chapter 19, verses 14-15 give more information about a white horse and a sword, "And the armies which were in heaven followed him upon white horses; And out of his mouth goeth a sharp sword, and with it he should smite the nations."

The meaning of His twoedged sword is suggested throughout other parts of Revelation. One edge is that his Word will lead the forces of Goodness to destroy those who challenge His existence as explained in Chapter 10. (This information was detailed in my previous article.) Christ's earthly warriors will be led by one described in Chapter 9, verse 11 as Abaddon or Apollyon, which are interpreted as the Destroyer. My current belief is, if this happens soon, that Donald Trump will be the one called upon to serve that purpose.

My interpretation of the other edge of that sword 'from His mouth' refers to Words from the pulpit that will help destroy that beast, Islam, by conversion. At these times many will be converted to accept God and Christ as the Son of God when they are forced, by His sword from His mouth to accept reality. Where are those warriors standing at the pulpit to wield the second edge of God's sword?

Article 74
Revelation's Monsters

Many who read Revelation interpret the information in Chapter 9 as describing horrible monsters that will attack humans on the earth during the end times. These monsters are described as scorpions, locusts, horses with crowns of gold, some having teeth as teeth of lions. Perhaps those who watch the national parade tomorrow will analyze those real military items as they really are; not as Apostle John saw them in his visions of the future as they came out of the smoke of that 'bottomless pit.'

That bottomless pit is John's definition of warfare. Real warfare does create much fire and smoke, which is endless until the battle subsides. If the graphics are realistic tomorrow just observe as aircraft appear from a distance that they could be interpreted as clouds of locusts. As you see the helicopters hover try to imagine how John would have seen them as scorpions of the earth that torment men from their tails. Real scorpions have stingers on their tails; while helicopters spew forth firepower from their tails. John's descriptions of horses with teeth like lions clearly describe battlefield vehicles that have large grills to allow a cooling airflow over the powerful engines. Those 'crowns of gold on their heads' clearly describe headgear of modern warriors.

If you have read Chapter 9 and watch the national parade tomorrow just imagine Apostle John trying to describe these things, from his visions, which he had never seen. How would we have described them in John's time? While watching that event enjoy the representation of our national protection from God and the great respect that each real American citizen has for each other.

Article 75
Watching our House

Many of my facebook friends know that the 'beast' in Revelation refers to Islam who rides that red horse described in Chapter 6, verse 4; and "power was given to him that sat thereon to take peace from the earth, and that they should kill one another: and there was given unto him a great sword." We don't know exactly when their great attack to take peace from the earth will happen; but, it will happen suddenly, "as a thief in the night" as two verses confirm.

As I watched the video of Iranians removing an unexploded mine from a ship they had attacked at night, hidden in the darkness, I immediately recalled the two verses about 'a thief in the night.' These are those verses:

Revelation 16:15, "Behold, I come as a thief. Blessed is he that watcheth, and keepeth his garments, lest he walk naked, and they see his shame."

1 Thessalonians 5:2, "For yourselves know perfectly that the day of the Lord so cometh as a thief in the night."

Matthew 24:43 adds, "But know this, that if the goodman of the house had known in what watch the thief would come, he would have watched, and would not have suffered his house to be broken up. 44) Therefore be ye also ready; for in such an hour as he think not the Son of man cometh."

Does this prophesy of 'coming as a thief in the night' refer to an action at night that will begin God's wrath against the beast, or does it mean He will come when we are not expecting His arrival? In either case, that beast, Islam, is already trying to hide his activities against the world 'as a thief in the night.'

https://www.theguardian.com/us-news/2019/jun/13/mike-pompeo-iran-gulf-oil-tanker-attacks

Article 76
More Understanding

How can anyone in their right mind, today, challenge the Words and validity of the Bible; especially the specific prophesy of Revelation? It's the last book of the Bible for a reason. That reason is to explain what will happen if the Words of God are not respected.

Growing stronger every day is the influence of those who mock Christianity in their efforts to turn true believers away from the truth. A clear example was Obama's comment, "We are no longer a Christian nation; at least not just." Since he made that statement many others have followed his lead to also convince us that Christianity is just one things of many to consider. In some cases they just simply mock Christians as those who flounder in the dark.

Revelation begins with a warning against this falling away by being influenced by 'false prophets and false apostles.' He even uses 'Jezebel' as an example of the pressure to be led away from God's word. His warning at the end of each of those 'Seven Letters' is "He that hath an ear, let him hear what the Spirit saith unto the churches." This includes every person even today.

Then Chapter 12 gets even more specific when it details the beginning of Christianity and the evil one, Satan, who tries to destroy Christ and His followers. It begins with Herod's failed attempts to kill Jesus. Then the story becomes very clear using the code of 'time, times, and half a time and 'a thousand two hundred and threescore days.' This becomes approximately three and a half years and three hundred and fifty years. This code reveals events that were to follow.

To hide from Herod Jesus and His family stayed in Egypt three and a half years, until Herod died. When they returned to Israel it was still under harsh rule for approximately 350 years at which time Constantine the Great of Rome (two wings of a great eagle) accepted and protected Christians for another 350 years. That put the time line at approximately 700 AD. That was the time Rome was kicked out of the Middle East by the new Muslim rulers with the rise of the Ottoman Empire. Jerusalem remained under Islamic rule until the 67' war when Israel regained control. To help maintain peace, Israel relinquished control of the Temple Mount to the Muslims; which will perhaps result in that being the 'Abomination of Desolation' sitting in the Holy Place. The Islamic Dome of the Rock sits atop Mount

Moriah.

Chapter 13 gives even more specific information facts that clearly identify Satan's two beasts; the antichrist and the second beast. This information will be explained in my next article.

With the clarity and specificity of this Biblical information there should be no doubt that these events written centuries before they happened are valid and reinforce that these written Words are Truth.

Article 77
Revelation's Seven Heads

This is the introductory comment from my last post: 'Chapter 13 gives even more specific information facts that clearly identify Satan's two beasts; the antichrist and the second beast.' This information is a continuation from that last article:

Chapter 13 in Revelation introduces and describes three beasts. The first two verses reveal the major beast with seven heads given 'power, and his seat, and great authority' by Satan. Other verses in Revelation identify this beast as Islam, the tool of Satan. The remaining verses in Chapter 13 identify the other two beasts; the first beast (the antichrist) and the second beast (the false prophet.)

This first beast is revealed as Muhammad by two specific identifications from other sources which are consolidated in 'The Timeline of Muhammad.' Verse 3 identifies this first beast as being wounded to death but was healed. This is an entry from 'The Battle of Uhud' that explains that event:

"The battle was fought on Saturday, 23 March 625 (7 Shawwal AH 3 in the Islamic calendar) at the valley located in front of Mount Uhud ---- But afterward, his archers left their position for the sake of plunder, thus allowing the enemy to attack the Muslims in the rear and surround them. The Prophet lost the day and very nearly lost his life. He was struck down by a shower of stones and wounded in the face by two arrows, and one of his front teeth was broken."

Then verse 5 reveals an even more specific identification of Muhammad as this beast. "And power was given unto him to continue forty and two months." The timeline of Muhammad reveals he was poisoned in 628 AD and died in 632. Notice the word 'continues' in this extract:

"632 AD Death of Muhammad. Muhammad's last days are spent with Aisha in her house, where he continues to issue orders and curse the Christians and Jews. Slumped against her bosom, he finally dies on the 8th of July."

Isn't it also interesting that this time uses the same code of time, times, and half a time as the codes interpreted in my last article? Forty-two months is three and a half years; that same time, times, and half a time. That 'second beast' will be discussed in my next article.

https://wikiislam.net/wiki/The_Timeline_of_Muhammad

Article 78
The Timeline of Muhammad.

Date and Event. All dates are approximate:

570 AD: Birth of Muhammad. Muhammad ibn 'Abdullah is born in "the year of the Elephant". His father, 'Abdu'llah ibn 'Abdu'l-Muttalib, had died before his birth, and his mother, Amina bint Wahb, swiftly puts him into the care of a wet-nurse named Halimah.

575 AD: Returned to mother. Believing that the young Muhammad is possessed by a demon, Halima returns him to his mother.

577 AD: Death of mother. After his mother's death, Muhammad is taken in by his grandfather, Abd al-Muttalib. And after his death, his paternal uncle, Abu Talib.

595 AD: Marriage to Khadijah. Muhammad marries his wealthy twice-divorced distant cousin, Khadijah, who later becomes his first follower. She had already borne two sons and a daughter from her previous marriages, and the union between her and the "insignificant" Muhammad is a controversial one which almost leads to bloodshed.

610 AD: The first "revelation." Muhammad receives what he comes to believe is his first otherworldly visitation, which he later identifies with the angel Jibreel (Gabriel) and a revelation from Allah. At first, he believes he may be possessed by a demon, and attempts to commit suicide, only to be stopped by the angel.

613 AD: Islam preached publicly. For the first time, Muhammad begins to preach Islam publicly in Mecca. His preaching is met with skepticism, and he is accused of plagiarizing the "tales of the ancients". One of his most sternest of critics is his own uncle, Abu Lahab, who is cursed by name in the Qur'an. The Meccans ask for miracles, but Muhammad gives them none.

615 AD: Friction with the Quraysh. Muhammad's "shameful" attacks on the native pagan beliefs causes friction between his followers and the Quraysh. Muhammad allows Muslims to leave Arabia for Abyssinia, while he chooses to stay behind and continue his preaching.

619 AD: Khadijah's death. The death of his wealthy and only wife Khadijah, is quickly followed by the death of his uncle and protector, Abu Talib. Not long after, he asks Abu Bakr for his six-year-old daughters hand in marriage.

619 AD: The Satanic verses incident. Muhammad finally acknowledges Allat, Manat, and al-Uzza, the goddesses of the pagan Meccans in a revelation. Upon hearing this, the Meccans are overjoyed. Later, following an alleged visit from the angel Jibreel, Muhammad recants and claims they were the words of the devil.

620 AD: Buraq and the Night Journey. Muhammad reports that he had been carried to Jerusalem and then to Paradise on a mythological flying steed named Buraq, and has met the other prophets. Over the sixth heaven, he meets Moses who weeps because there would be more Muslims in heaven than Jews.

622 AD: The Hijra. Due to growing animosity between the pagan and Muslim Meccans, Muhammad and his followers flee to Medina, marking the beginning of the Hijra era of the Islamic lunar calender, and also paving the way for Muhammad's metamorphosis from a preacher to a political and military leader.

622 AD: Marriage consummation with Aisha. Muhammad consummates his marriage to Aisha, his nine-year-old bride. Originally when Muhammad had asked for Aisha's hand in marriage, her father, Abu Bakr, had protested.

624 AD: The Nakhla raid. Muhammad orders the 7th Caravan Raid against the pagan Meccans, a raid which would mark the beginning of violence in the name of Islam. Taking place in one of the four holy months in which fighting was forbidden, the leader of the Meccan caravan is killed, and two others are taken captive.

624 AD: The Battle of Badr. Following the caravan raids, the Meccans decide to retaliate. Although they're vastly outnumbered, the Muslims defeat the pagan Meccans; killing at least seventy and capturing another seventy for ransom. Among the prisoners of war is Al Nadir, a storyteller and poet who had mocked Muhammad. Ali beheads Al Nadir on Muhammad's orders. Muhammad also orders another twenty-four to be thrown into the well of Badr.

624 AD: Exile of the Jewish Qaynuqa. Breaking an earlier treaty, Muhammad and the Muslims besiege the Jewish Qaynuqa tribe. Muhammad initially intends to execute all the males, but following an emotional plea from Abdullah bin Ubayy, he confiscates their property and exiles them from Medina.

625 AD: The Battle of Uhud.   The second military encounter between the Meccans (led by Abu Sufyan) and the Muslims. Due to the Muslim focus on salvaging booty rather than victory,[14] this time the pagan Meccans defeat the Muslims of Medina, and Muhammad himself is hurt by an attack from Khalid ibn al-Walid.

625 AD: Siege and exile of the Jewish Nadir. The Muslim siege of the Jewish Nadir tribe lasts for two weeks, after which they surrender. Muhammad confiscates their weapons and exiles them from Medina.

627 AD: The Battle of the Trench. The Battle of the Trench was not a battle at all, but a fortnight-long siege. Having heard of the strength of the approaching Meccan army, Muhammad's companion, Salman the Persian, advises him there should be trenches dug around the northern front of Medina to prevent hostile Meccans from entering Muslim territory. Coming unprepared for a siege, the Meccan army retreat after two weeks.

627 AD: The Genocide of the Jewish Qurayza. Following the Battle of the Trench, Muhammad accuses the Jews of Banu Qurayza of betraying him. The women and young children who have not yet reached puberty are taken captive by Muslims to be sold in slave markets for horses and weapons, and all the males who have reached puberty are beheaded on Muhammad's orders.

628 AD: The Treaty of Hudaybiyya. Muhammad and his men attempt to make a pilgrimage to Mecca. His forces are met outside the city by the pagan Meccans. Muhammad and the pagan Meccans conclude the Treaty of Hudaybiyya, a ten-year truce.

628 AD: The conquest of Khaybar. Muhammad and the Muslims besiege the Khaybar oasis. The combatants killed, and the women and children allotted as booty. The Jewish leader, Kinana, is tortured and beheaded, and his young widow, Safiyah, is taken by Muhammad for himself.

628 AD. Poisoned at Khaybar. Immediately following the conquest of Khaybar, Muhammad and his men are served a meal of poisoned lamb by a Jewish women named Zaynab bint al-Harith, causing him to fall ill. Muhammad questions her, and then has her executed.

630 AD: The conquest of Mecca. The Muslims conquer Mecca. Muhammad rides on camel-back to the Ka'aba, then starts reciting verses from the Qur'an, while his men remove and destroy everything they consider idolatrous from the Ka'aba. This is the first of many non-Muslim worship places to be forcibly converted into a mosque.

630 AD: Muhammad rules Arabia. The Muslims prevail in the Battle of Hunayn against the Bedouin tribe of Hawazin and conquer Ta'if. In doing so, they capture huge spoils, consisting of 6,000 women and children and 24,000 camels. Muhammad is now the ruler of Arabia.

631 AD: All Arabians submit to Islam. Muhammad sends (the now converted) Khalid ibn al-Walid and other warriors to the remaining non-Muslim Arabian tribes, forcing them to accept Islam.

631 AD: The Tabuk raid. The expedition to Tabuk marked the first real act of aggression by the Muslims against Christians. Two/thirds of the Christian world would be conquered before the much belated and weak response of the crusades. By the time Muhammad arrives

at Tabuk, the Byzantine troops have already withdrawn. However, the local Christian leaders are forced to pay Jizyah and submit to Islamic rule.

632 AD: The Farewell pilgrimage. After completion of the pilgrimage, Muhammad delivers his famous sermon which leads to the commencement of the conquests against the Christians and Zoroastrians.

632 AD: Death of Muhammad. Muhammad's last days are spent with Aisha in her house, where he continues to issue orders and curse the Christians and Jews. Slumped against her bosom, he finally dies on the 8th of July. Ali (Muhammad's son-in-law and cousin) reports that Muhammad's penis was erect after his death.

Article 79
The Second Beast

Chapter 13 in Revelation identifies a beast with seven heads rising up out of the sea (sea of mankind.) One of his heads, the first beast, was identified in my last article as the antichrist, Muhammad. The word 'antichrist' is never used in Revelation. Verse 10 then describes the death of this first beast "he that killeth with the sword must be killed with the sword." The remaining verses in Chapter 13 then refer to the rise and activity of the second beast, also identified in Chapters 19 and 20 as the 'false prophet.'

Verse 11, "And I beheld another beast coming up out of the earth, and he had two horns like a lamb, and he spake as a dragon." This clearly means that he claimed to be a Christian, but he spoke words supporting Satan's army, Islam. This is indicated in Chapter 17, verse 3 as 'a woman sitting upon a scarlet colored beast having seven heads and ten horns.' Revelation introduces only two women (religions: Christianity and Islam.) Barack Obama claimed to be a Christian but his praise was all for Islam; fulfilling this part of the prophesy.

The next verses reveal that he had the same power as the first beast, meaning he had the same leadership authority as Muhammad; the leader of a nation and a large following. Verse 13 suggests he used aerial firepower (by great wonders he made fire come down from the sky) to deceptively allow the growth of ISIS and other warriors for Islam to create a stronger foothold in the Middle East. While ISIS was growing he even proclaimed that ISIS was a 'JV team' suggesting the dream of a caliphate in that region was insignificant. That growth of Islam was to become that life 'unto the image of the beast' suggested in verse 15. Not only did Obama support that image with deceptive firepower, he also aided that growth with much money. An extract from this article in the Washington Times By Bill Gertz, Wednesday, February 7, 2018 explains:

"The U.S. government has traced some of the $1.7 billion released to Iran by the Obama administration to Iranian-backed terrorists in the two years since the cash was transferred. According to knowledgeable sources, Iran has used the funds to pay its main proxy, the Lebanon-based terrorist group Hezbollah, along with the Quds Force, Iran's main foreign intelligence and covert action arm and element of the Islamic Revolutionary Guards Corps."

And there's even a more specific code that Barack Obama is this second beast. It's from verse 18: "Count the number of the beast; for it is the number of a man; and his number is Six hundred threescore and six." (666) The only way to count this number is to count 6+6+6 which is 18. Now count the letters in the name: BARACKHUSSEINOBAMA. Plus, the confirmation for this code and this number is that it's written in Verse 18.

Before the rise of Muhammad no one could have interpreted that part of Revelation. Before the rise of Barack Obama no one could have interpreted this part of Revelation. Now Revelation is made very clear; which makes the Words of the Bible very clear.

Article 80
Seven Deadly Sins

Some people ask, "What are the seven deadly sins?" The seven deadly sins viewed by society and literature are:

Lust – to have an intense desire or need: "But I tell you that anyone who looks at a woman lustfully has already committed adultery with her in his heart" (Matthew 5:28).

Gluttony – excess in eating and drinking: "for drunkards and gluttons become poor, and drowsiness clothes them in rags" (Proverbs 23:21).

Greed - excessive or reprehensible acquisitiveness: "Having lost all sensitivity, they have given themselves over to sensuality so as to indulge in every kind of impurity, with a continual lust for more" (Ephesians 4:19).

Laziness – disinclined to activity or exertion: not energetic or vigorous: "The way of the sluggard is blocked with thorns, but the path of the upright is a highway" (Proverbs 15:19).

Wrath – strong vengeful anger or indignation: "A gentle answer turns away wrath, but a harsh word stirs up anger" (Proverbs 15:1)

Envy – painful or resentful awareness of an advantage enjoyed by another joined with a desire to possess the same advantage: "Therefore, rid yourselves of all malice and all deceit, hypocrisy, envy, and slander of every kind. Like newborn babies, crave pure spiritual milk, so that by it you may grow up in your salvation" (1 Peter 2:1-2).

Pride - quality or state of being proud – inordinate self esteem: "Pride goes before destruction, a haughty spirit before a fall" (Proverbs 16:18).

What are the seven detestable sins according to the Bible?

"There are six things the Lord hates, seven that are detestable to him: haughty eyes, a lying tongue, hands that shed innocent blood, a heart that devises wicked schemes, feet that are quick to rush into evil, a false witness who pours out lies and a man who stirs up dissension among brothers" (Proverbs 6:16-19).

Article 81
Eyes of Satan

There are two 'seventh angels' described in Revelation. One is the angel who blows the seventh trumpet to warn of impending horrors. The other is the seventh angel described in Chapter 10. This angel is Satan. How do we know?

It begins in the first verse of Chapter 12, where a woman (the religion Christianity) came down from heaven with a crown of twelve stars. This 12 represents Christ's apostles. Then Satan drew a third of the stars of Heaven with him when he was removed from Heaven. A third of the total of 18 stars would be 6 stars, which represent angels. Including his six angels, Satan would be the seventh angel. Then the first verse in Chapter 13 begins to explain the rise of those seven angels and their war against God.

"And I stood upon the sand of the sea, and saw a beast rise up out of the sea, having seven heads and ten horns, and upon the horns ten crowns, and upon heads the name of blasphemy." In this case the 'sea' refers to the sea of humanity. The sand refers to the great population of the earth. Not only do these seven heads refer to Satan and his helpers, in another verse it's also described as the whole earth, meaning the seven continents. Only two of Satan's six angel helpers are identified.

The first is in verse 3 which identifies one of the seven heads as "wounded to death, and his deadly wound was healed." This is from Muhammad's great head wound at the Battle of Uhud in 625 AD.

Verse 5 also is written that he continued "forty and two months." Muhammad was poisoned in 628 AD and continued to function until 632. In our modern day I believe the spirit of another of those six angels lives in the body of Barack Hussein Obama. Verse 11, "And I beheld another beast coming up out of the earth, and he had two horns like a lamb, (claims to be a Christian) and he spake as a dragon (supports Islam and Satan.)"

This means that four more of Satan's angels continue to control the minds and beings of some who exist among us today. And perhaps we have a good clue as to who they might be. Have you noticed the similarity of the glaring eyes of Nancy Pelosi, Adam Schiff, and the newly-minted non-stop flapping mouth new congresswoman from New York? If these are three of that four wandering angel spirits who support Satan, where is the fourth one? Do those blaring, glaring eyes give a clue? Any ideas?

Article 82

Satan's Voice

Chapter 10 describes Satan's arrival on earth and his oath to remove God's time in Heaven. He and his angels spoke words for Apostle John to write in his Book of Revelation. John writes, "I was about to write: and I heard a voice from heaven saying unto me, Seal up those things which the seven thunders uttered, and write them not." So, why is it important to understand the significance of this seventh angel? Verse 7 explains the current relevance:

"But in the days of the voice of the seventh angel, when he shall begin to sound, the mystery of God should be finished."

That 'voice of the seventh angel' has begun to sound. It sounds in the voices and growing influence of Islam. Islam is Satan's warrior force that plans to fulfill Satan's oath by trying to remove God's time in heaven. Satan has sworn to do it, and Islam is his tool. That seventh angel has begun to sound and his sound is being accepted in more and more places. Satan has already begun to attack God's great blessings of many nations.

Article 83
Blinded by the Light

I just read a post asking the question; if we know Muslims are opposed to our way of life why are we electing them to political positions to harm us? It's also clear as 'light' that they are Satan's army to war against God in Heaven. That deceiver, that angel of light, is their guiding force. That's described in 2 Corinthians, Chapter 11, verses 13-15:

"For such are false apostles, deceitful workers, transforming themselves into the apostles of Christ. And no marvel, for Satan himself is transformed into an angel of light. Therefore it is no great thing if his ministers also be transformed as the minister of righteousness; whose end shall be according to their works."

The purpose for those seven letters to the seven churches in Asia, the first three chapters in Revelation, is to warn us against false apostles; those 'who say they are Jews, and are not, but are of the synagogue of Satan;' and to those "who sufferest that woman Jezebel, which calleth herself a prophetess, to teach and to seduce my servants to commit fornication, and to eat things sacrificed unto idols." This refers to those who claim Muhammad was 'the prophet' and who eat halal food sacrificed to a black rock in Mecca and who commit fornication with little underage girls. Jezebel is the synonym for the total of those false prophets.

Apostle John of Revelation also marveled at Islam's deception after identifying Islam in 13:6, "And I saw the woman (Islam) drunken with the blood of the saints and with the blood of the martyrs of Jesus: and when I saw her, I wondered with great admiration. (7) And the angel said unto me, Wherefore didst thou marvel?"

Too many today are 'marveled' by that angel of light and his ministers. Obviously, they refuse to open their eyes to see that light. At some point when it's too late for them, God will open their eyes.

Article 84
Give Me Free Stuff!

Recently I posted an article about being blinded by the light, referring to Islam's claim to be a religion of peace but is in reality guided by that 'angel of light' Satan. His goal is to destroy God's time in Heaven. We are also under attack by that same angel of light in another form. These attacks are guided by Satan's sworn oath, in Chapter 10 of Revelation, to war against God.

First, let's answer who is this angel of light. It's explained in Second Corinthians, verses 13-14: "For such are false apostles, deceitful workers, transforming themselves into apostles of Christ. And no marvel, for Satan himself is transformed into an angel of light." This angel of light concept applies to many situations, but how does it now specifically apply to the Democrats who are promoting their new 'light' of Socialism?

In our current age this movement began with Barack Obama's promise of everyone getting their fair share. Also, keep in mind that in my opinion he is also that 'second beast' of Revelation, Chapter 13, who claims to be a Christian but who praises only Muhammad and Islam. His influence continues to flourish deceptively in the minds of Satan's other angels. Doesn't this promise of a 'fair share' sound de'light'ful? But, hold on; there are Words against this idea.

Second Thessalonians gives a warning against waiting for this fair share, as those apostles of that angel of light promise the lazy and uninspired who only wait their turn to be fed. Chapter 3, verses 10-12: "For even when we were with you, this we commanded you, that if any would not work, neither should he eat. For we hear that there are some which walk among you disorderly, working not at all, but are busybodies. Now them that are such we command and exhort by our Lord Jesus Christ, that with quietness they work, and eat their own bread."

This brings forth an important question for those who follow that angel of light into those promises of Socialism. How hard will you work for you own bread if your bread is promised to you for free as a fair share?

Article 85
Those Darn Little Beasts

In two of my recent articles I mentioned the horrors that would happen when the fourth seal was opened that released that fourth horse of the Apocalypse, the pale horse with Death sitting on his back. It begins in Verse 7 of Chapter 6, "And when he had opened the fourth seal, I heard the voice of the fourth beast say, Come and see.

Verse 8 continues, "And I looked, and behold a pale horse: and his name that sat on him was Death, and Hell followed with him. And power was given unto them over the fourth part of the earth, to kill with sword, and with hunger, and with death, and with the beasts of the earth." The first two, sword and hunger, were detailed in those two articles. But what about 'death' and 'beasts?'

Perhaps by 'death' means natural death such as heart attacks, cancer, diabetes and many of those natural problems that now are somewhat controlled by medicines or other remedies. If our global economy is destroyed or severely limited, as described in Chapter 18, these needed remedies and procedures would not be available for many people across the world. Many would be left to suffer a slow and agonizing death.

By 'beasts' is another consideration. My vision for many months was 'how could that many beasts escape from zoos and other places to present that large hazard across the world.' As I was pondering that question I suffered a strong mosquito bite. That's when the obvious jumped right in my face. Those beasts are not the large ferocious beasts of the earth; they are those little beasts you can't see when they sneak up on you and often take that horrible bite. More of those beasts exist in the form of ticks, wasps, snakes, and spiders. They are sneaky little beasts that can cause death.

The books of Daniel, Matthew and Revelation reveal these hazards could last from three and a half to seven years. Perhaps a good stock of insect repellant should be considered before that time arrives.

Article 86
What's for Dinner?

A previous article discussed Revelation's prophetic warning about things that would occur before that great battle of Armageddon. As a reminder, Armageddon is not the last war, since there will be a thousand years of peace (without war) before that battle of Gog and Magog. And, as wormwood, the use and importance of drugs, gives us a clue of time; so does another prophesy from 2 Timothy, Chapter 3, verses 1-5:

"This know also, that in the last days perilous times shall come. For men shall be lovers of their own selves, covetous, boasters, proud, blasphemers, disobedient to parents, unthankful, unholy, without natural affection, trucebreakers, false accusers, incontinent, fierce, despisers of those that are good, traitors, heady, highminded, lovers of pleasures more than lovers of God; Having a form of godliness, but denying the power thereof: from such turn away." Two of these are very clear today:

First is 'despisers of those that are good.' Is this not a clear and perfect description of those who hate and 'despise' Donald Trump so fiercely they would sacrifice our great nation to destroy him? Second is 'having a form of godliness, but denying the power thereof.' Does this not describe the new acceptance of Islam as one of the three Abrahamic religions; although Islam is determined to do Satan's will and destroy all Christians and others who worship the real God? Now let's return to that prophesy of the Apocalyptic pale horse.

The next danger identified is hunger, food and thirst, during that time of tribulation. Daniel identified this as seven years; the same time as in ancient Israel when Joseph and his brothers went to Egypt during a drought for wheat. The rider of the third horse, the black horse, also mentions the cost of wheat and barley. Matthew reveals that half that tribulation will be a great tribulation. So perhaps only that three and a half years will be our time of greatest hardship. It's possible that those who live on land that can grow crops can survive without much hunger. Others in extreme urban areas will likely suffer the greatest hunger conditions; obviously many will die.

Each person and family must cope with this disaster. The great caution is not to wait until all the store shelves are empty; and most grocery store shelves are stocked with only a three day supply. Be prepared.

Article 87
Where are the Bullets?

Revelation reveals that seven trumpets were introduced when the seventh seal, that last seal, was opened. These trumpets introduced warfare and activities connected to warfare; that is all except the third trumpet. Chapter 8 explains what happened when the first four trumpets were sounded by angels. This third trumpet interrupted the war scenes and introduced a great star Wormwood that caused many men to die. This wormwood is a synonym, a representation, of the increasing hazard of drugs. Wormwood is a wild plant that produces a drug. Wormwood has already fallen upon us. The fourth trumpet introduces three woes of warfare. The warriors and equipment for that great war are detailed in Chapter 9.

It's unlikely that we in America will be directly affected when that flash point of war begins in the Middle East as mentioned in another article. That article also described the lack of ships on the sea and the transport of items now dependant on world trade and world markets. Some items we need for our daily activities will not be available. This includes equipment, repair parts for equipment, daily use items and even some food. Interdependent world trade could severely disrupt our modern way of life, including safety and security. Many of these items are detailed in Chapter18.

Perhaps this could create the condition described when that fourth horse of the Apocalypse, the pale horse, appears. Death rides on his back. (Chapter 6, verse 8) "And power was given unto them over the fourth part of the earth, to kill with sword, and with hunger, and with death, and with the beasts of the earth." Should we possibly consider some preparation just in case? And what's the first clue of preparation? The sword is first on the list so let's consider that first.

The sword represents death by violence. Therefore we must be prepared to defend ourselves in a world that might be unable to defend individual citizens. For example, we have been warned of the great danger of drugs, that wormwood. How desperate would users be to continue their great need? Would they invade your home to get your possessions to support that need? In the process would they kill you and your family? If you are against the ownership of private guns perhaps you might reconsider. Is your opinion more important than the lives of your spouse and children?

If you decide to be prepared, there's another caution; don't wait too late. In the scare during Obama's administration weapons and ammunition flew off the shelves. Some ammunition was unavailable for months, especially .22 caliber. Just imagine the lack of domestic ammunition if a great war suddenly begins in the Middle East.

Article 88

Babylon is Fallen

Are we nearing that time of tribulation revealed in the Books of Daniel, Matthew and Revelation? I can't answer this question definitively, but I have researched many signs that suggest those hardships are not far away. Of course, our distance from the flash point, the Middle East, will protect us somewhat, but here in

America we will still have many uncomfortable times during the event. This clue is given in Revelation, Chapter 18, by the mention of ships on the sea and the profits from ocean trade. These verses refer to that great event:

Verse 2 states that "Babylon the great is fallen, is fallen, and is become the habitation of devils, and the hold of every foul spirit, and a cage of every unclean and hateful bird." Babylon the great is defined in Chapter 17 as the woman (religion) Islam. Verse 3 continues, "For all nations have drunk of the wine of the wrath of her fornication, and the kings of the earth have committed fornication with her, and the merchants of the earth are waxed rich through the abundance of her delicacies." (Unfortunately, even the Pope has welcomed Islam into his realm.)

Verse 9 continues, revealing that the earth shall lament for her (Babylon) 'when they shall see the smoke of her burning.' Verses 10-11 continue, "Standing afar off for the fear of her torment, saying, alas, alas that great city Babylon, that mighty city! For in one hour is thy judgment come. And the merchants of the earth shall weep and mourn over her; for no man buyeth their merchandise any more."

So here in the United States what will be a great sign that the Great War is beginning? It seems this sign will be when nations around Israel begin a major attack. And, even now Hamas, Syria, and Iran are assembling that horrible army for that attack. This includes the recent longer range missile tests by Iran. For what other reason would Iran (ancient Persia) want greater missiles?

Article 89
Where Are They?

Where Are the Voices of Our Christian Leaders?

As many who read my blogs and articles know, I am trying to share as many of those messages in Revelation as I can interpret. I read, study, and research these Words almost every day and try to share that little knowledge that I sometime gain. But I realize that my messages are small and limited; for I am not the one trained to be expressing and exposing these things, especially that great and determined threat by Satan through the actions of his current army, Islam and others, to destroy God and His believers. Our responsible and knowledgeable church leaders must be the leaders in this role. Where are they at this great time of pending peril?

Most Christians know how to be responsible, love one another, and worship God and His Son Jesus Christ. This seems to be the only message we get from our church leaders today. Of course that's a wonderful and Godly message and a needed reminder, but it's not the only message we need today. That 'seventh angel' described in Revelation, Chapter 10, has begun to sound and our Christian leaders are letting him have his way without interruption. That 'seventh angel' in Chapter 10 is Satan who has vowed to remove God's time in Heaven; verse 7:

"But in the days of the voice of the seventh angel, when he shall begin to sound, the mystery of God should be finished, as he hath declared to his servants the prophets."

Please read and re-read this Chapter 10 to understand Satan's vowed threat. The voice of this seventh angel is not only sounding all around us today, his voice is shouting in every nook and corner of our society.

Where are the voices of our church leaders to curtail the voice of Satan and his growing number of dedicated followers who have vowed to defeat God? They must come out and express God's Word even louder and clearer than the voice of that seventh angel. Where are they?

Article 90
Donald Trump's Colors

Donald Trump's remarks about athletes (kneeling) standing up for the flag and for the national anthem have nothing to do with the colors of racism; black and white. His comments have everything to do with the colors of Red, White, and Blue. These are the colors of our flag; blessed by the Grace of God. These colors also represent our nation's idealism.

The color of White represents the idealism under which our nation strives to fulfill the concept that 'All men are created equal, on a pure and clean playing field.'

The color of Red represents the blood and sorrows shed by millions of our nation's heros; military, police, and first responders, who give their lives and blood to protect that white banner of idealism and freedom. Their family members see that red color daily of their relatives killed in honor of that Red, White, and Blue.

The color of Blue represents the open sky of possibilities and opportunities of success for any citizen of our Red, White, and Blue nation who chooses to reach that unlimited dream by personal effort to achieve his or her aspiration. That includes the individual choice, for many, to have no aspirations; those who complain most because they have no guiding light. They can't see that color Blue.

That Red, White, and Blue represents the heritage, freedom, and opportunity for each and every individual in America to fulfill that goal for which it stands; if each individual chooses that course for his or her life. It's an individual and personal decision. As Donald Trump exemplifies; it's not a choice made by the colors of black and white.

God bless America; and keep that Red, White and Blue flying over us. And may God protect Donald Trump from the many who hate our Red, White, and Blue who wish to destroy him and our great nation.

Conclusion

Many events are taking place today that create great stress and division on our great nation. America was founded on the principle and concept of 'One Nation Under God.' With that foundation, America rose quickly to become the greatest nation the world has ever known.

Not only did America become the powerful and influential beacon of world protection, we also rose to the pinnacle of attraction for anyone seeking happiness, prosperity and fulfillment. Then America became complacent in its ability and accomplishments. A great and dangerous fissure rose when those among us turned their vision from the Grace of God to fulfill more visions of personal power; even to the levels of world domination; having a self-appointed god to lead the great new one-world order.

That great status of freedom for all changed to 'don't worry about your self-determination and self-destiny; let me take care of you and I will be your god to point the way for you.' This is the basic tenant of socialism. Those who are lazy and 'unwilling to earn their own bread' traded their souls for this promise of free bread which allowed those new self-appointed gods to rule their lives. In that quest a great chasm arose which has divided our nation.

Although this determination by those self-appointed gods to lead us is not a new divide; the proponents of that effort seem to have more influence with an even greater following. This is one source of great danger to America and our freedom, it's not the only deep threat. That chasm created by socialism has allowed two other major dangers to arise from that abyss. One is the direct threat by Islam to destroy God's blessing for the world by deadly force; terrorism. The other is the insidious encroachment by Islam to conquer the world with the process of Settlement; that is to sneak into our nation until their population is strong enough to consume us politically.

In either case of Islam's effort to destroy our way of life they have but one goal. That goal is to make everyone on earth a Muslim; or dead. This is the message clearly revealed in that Bible Book of Revelation. It seems however, that from the Words, their hate is so great against everything that even if they were to become the only religion left on Earth they would then destroy one another; as prophesied by that 'red horse' with one rider that kills one another.

This book was written to accomplish three major goals. First, was to demonstrate that the Book of Revelation was not written by Apostle John as a demonstration of his wild imagination or visions. His prophesies from the Words and visions from God have become true and valid. John could not have imagined by himself those times and events of reality. This demonstrates that things John prophesied to happen in the near future are destined to happen. The overall caution to each of us to be prepared.

The second goal is to warn everyone of the great danger of Islam's determination to dominate the world. It's their religion of Satan, therefore they will stop at nothing to accomplish that goal. The mother of that religion, Babylon the Great, feigns love and peace while she allows and guides her harlots and terrorists to wreak death and destruction. God's common warning to those seven churches in Asia, and to all who accept His word, is, "He that hath an ear, let him hear what the Spirit saith unto the churches."

Finally, my prayer is that all who love our great nation strive to return America again 'Under God' so that our strength of character and strength of nation will be so great that no one or no religion would dare attack our nation or our ideals. At the moment it seems Donald Trump has been the one appointed to protect those things we cherish. Hopefully, when that great attack happens the great hate and war against him will be remolded into a common cause and he will be given cooperation and support to defeat that deep state and that Babylon the Great who is determined to destroy us.

God bless America

About the Author

Will Clark's author experiences began by writing inspection and evaluation reports in the U.S. Air Force. He is a retired Air Force officer and a Vietnam veteran, serving in Saigon from 1966 to 1967. His other overseas assignments include Misawa, Japan and Ankara, Turkey; where he visited the ancient sites of the Seven Churches.

In 1995, as a 'Friends of Education' study skills project, he authored a book, How to Learn, to encourage students to improve their grades in DeSoto County, Mississippi. Education supporters printed and distributed four thousand copies. The following school year he wrote a weekly education column for a local newspaper, The DeSoto County Tribune. He also taught an adult GED class. His book, How to Learn, has been updated and is now available everywhere.

His next published book was School Bells and Broken Tales, a parody of nursery rhyme characters, also a motivation and education book for children. Other books include Shades of Retribution, a historical novel, and Simply Success, a motivation guide for students and employees.

His action novel, The Atlantis Crystal, is the first of a trilogy based on Atlantis and crystals. The other two books are: She Waits in Atlantis, and Return to Atlantis. This trilogy is based on his travels while assigned to Turkey, site of the ancient city of Troy. His latest political thriller is: America 20XX: The New World Order.

The past five years he has devoted his full time to the study, research, and writing of an analysis of the Book of Revelation and the danger of Satan, that beast that guides Islam.

Things We Must Never Forget

Benghazi

Why were four Americans killed?
Where was Hillary Clinton while it was happening?
Where was Barack Obama while it was happening?
Why did they lie and blame the event on a video?
Why were rescuers on 'stand by' told to 'stand down?'

Fast and Furious

Who authorized the operation?
Why did the operation continue after weapons were lost?
Why did the procedure have no procedure?
Why weren't tracking devices used?

The IRS Scandal

What was the highest level involved?
Who initiated it?
Why hasn't anyone been fired or reprimanded?
What dangers could be unleashed by this organization?

Greatest Quotes
of Our Time

Michelle Obama
February 18, 2008
"For the first time in my adult life I am proud of my country."
(Age 44)

Barack Obama
March 9, 2008"We are no longer a Christian nation - at least not just."
September 25, 2012
Remarks to the UN General Assembly
"The future must not belong to those who slander Islam."

Nancy Pelosi
March 9, 2010
"We have to pass the bill so that you can find out what is in it."

Hillary Clinton
January 23, 2013
"What difference, at this point, does it make?"
December 3, 2014
"...showing respect even for one's enemies, trying to understand and insofar as psychologically possible, empathize with their perspective and point of view."

Other Books by the Author

Novels
Shades of Retribution
The Atlantis Crystal
She Waits in Atlantis
Return to Atlantis
America 20XX: The New World Order
666: Mark of the Beast
Death Drones: 2025

Children's Books:
Forest Trails and Fairy Tales
Wishing Wells and Broken Tales
Student Study Skills
American Heroes: Students Who Learn

Non-Fiction:
Simply Success
The Education Jungle
How to Learn
The Day America Died
Obama's Ring: The Seat of Satan
Managing Without Conflict
The Peer Pressure Monster
Obama, Hillary, Saul Alinsky and Their Useful Idiots
Denied 3 Times

The War on Christians
Who is the Antichrist
Islamic Two-Headed Beast
Islam Attacks the Whore
The Second Beast
Secrets of the Seven Churches
Two Woman of the Apocalypse
Islam's Bloodthirsty Sword
Once Upon A Revelation: About Islam
America Gasps
God's Islamaknowbe Warriors
Who is the Antichrist Beast?
Who is the False Prophet Beast?
Who is the Woman Jezebel?
Who is Babylon the Great?
What is the Tribulation?
Apocalypse 2019: Created by Jezebel, Muhammad and Barack Obama
Obama Rides A Scarlet Red Beast
Secret Codes of Revelation
Islam is That Beast
Trump, Apollyon, and Obama
A Reason to Believe

Attachment 1
Hillary Clinton Background

Hillary Clinton's association with Saul Alinsky began early in her life, while she was in school. This information from Freebeacon.com introduces the beginning of that relationship. The article was submitted by Alana Goodman on 21 September, 2014:

"Previously unpublished correspondence between Hillary Clinton and the late left-wing organizer Saul Alinsky reveals new details about her relationship with the controversial Chicago activist and shed light on her early ideological development.

Clinton met with Alinsky several times in 1968 while writing a Wellesley college thesis about his theory of community organizing. Clinton's relationship with Alinsky, and her support for his philosophy, continued for several years after she entered Yale law school in 1969, two letters obtained by the Washington Free Beacon show.

The letters obtained by the Free Beacon are part of the archives for the Industrial Areas Foundation, a training center for community organizers founded by Alinsky, which are housed at the University of Texas at Austin. The letters also suggest that Alinsky, who died in 1972, had a deeper influence on Clinton's early political views than previously known.

A 23-year-old Hillary Clinton was living in Berkeley, California, in the summer of 1971. She was interning at the left-wing law firm Treuhaft, Walker and Burnstein, known for its radical politics and a client roster that included Black Panthers and other militants.

On July 8, 1971, Clinton reached out to Alinsky, then 62, in a letter sent via airmail, paid for with stamps featuring Franklin Delano

Roosevelt, and marked "Personal."

"Dear Saul," she began. "When is that new book [Rules for Radicals] coming out—or has it come and I somehow missed the fulfillment of Revelation?"

"I have just had my one-thousandth conversation about Reveille [for Radicals] and need some new material to throw at people," she added, a reference to Alinsky's 1946 book on his theories of community organizing.

Clinton devoted just one paragraph in her memoir Living History to Alinsky, writing that she rejected a job offer from him in 1969 in favor of going to law school. She wrote that she wanted to follow a more conventional path.

However, in the 1971 letter, Clinton assured Alinsky that she had "survived law school, slightly bruised, with my belief in and zest for organizing intact."

"The more I've seen of places like Yale Law School and the people who haunt them, the more convinced I am that we have the serious business and joy of much work ahead—if the commitment to a free and open society is ever going to mean more than eloquence and frustration," wrote Clinton.

According to the letter, Clinton and Alinsky had kept in touch since she entered Yale. The 62-year-old radical had reached out to give her advice on campus activism.

"If I never thanked you for the encouraging words of last spring in the midst of the Yale-Cambodia madness, I do so now," wrote Clinton, who had moderated a campus election to join an anti-war student strike.

She added that she missed their regular conversations, and asked if Alinsky would be able to meet her the next time he was in California.

"I am living in Berkeley and working in Oakland for the summer and would love to see you," Clinton wrote. "Let me know if there is any chance of our getting together."

Clinton's letter reached Alinsky's office while he was on an extended trip to Southeast Asia, where he was helping train community organizers in the Philippines.

But a response letter from Alinsky's secretary suggests that the radical organizer had a deep fondness for Clinton as well.

"Since I know [Alinsky's] feelings about you I took the liberty of opening your letter because I didn't want something urgent to wait for two weeks," Alinsky's long-time secretary, Georgia Harper, wrote to Clinton in a July 13, 1971 letter. "And I'm glad I did."

Harper told Clinton that Alinksy's book Rules for Radicals had been released. She enclosed several reviews of the book.

"Mr. Alinsky will be in San Francisco, staying at the Hilton Inn at the airport on Monday and Tuesday, July 26 and 27," Harper added. "I know he would like to have you call him so that if there is a chance in his schedule maybe you can get together."

It is unclear whether the meeting occurred.

A self-proclaimed radical, Alinsky advocated guerilla tactics and civil disobedience to correct what he saw as an institutionalized power gap in poor communities. His philosophy divided the world into "haves"—middle class and wealthy people —and "have nots"—the poor. He took an ends-justify-the-means approach to power and wealth redistribution, and developed the theoretical basis of "community organizing."

"The Prince was written by Machiavelli for the Haves on how to hold power," wrote Alinsky in his 1971 book. "Rules for Radicals is written for the Have-Nots on how to take it away."

Clinton's connection to Alinsky has been the subject of speculation for decades. It became controversial when Wellsley College, by request of the Clinton White House, sealed her 1968 thesis from the public for years. Conservative lawyer Barbara Olson said Clinton had asked for the thesis to be sealed because it showed "the extent to which she internalized and assimilated the beliefs and methods of Saul Alinsky." Clinton opponent turned Clinton defender David Brock referred to her as "Alinsky's daughter" in 1996's The Seduction of Hillary Rodham.

The paper was opened to the public in 2001. While the thesis is largely sympathetic to Alinsky, it is also critical of some of his tactics.

Clinton described the organizer as "a man of exceptional charm," but also objected to some of the conflicts he provoked as "unrealistic," noting that his model could be difficult for others to replicate.

"Many of the Alinsky-inspired poverty warriors could not (discounting political reasons) move beyond the cathartic first step of organizing groups 'to oppose, complain, demonstrate, and boycott' to developing and running a program," she wrote.

The letters obtained by the Free Beacon suggest that Clinton experimented more with radical politics during her law school years than she has publicly acknowledged.

In Living History, she describes her views during that time as far more pragmatic than leftwing.

She "agreed with some of Alinsky's ideas," Clinton wrote in her first memoir, but the two had a "fundamental disagreement" over his anti-establishment tactics.

She described how this disagreement led to her parting ways with

Alinsky in the summer before law school in 1969.

"He offered me the chance to work with him when I graduated from college, and he was disappointed that I decided instead to go to law school," she wrote.

"Alinsky said I would be wasting my time, but my decision was an expression of my belief that the system could be changed from within."

A request for comment from the Clinton team was not returned.

The author of this article, Alana Goodman, is a staff writer for the Washington Free Beacon. Prior to joining the Beacon, she was assistant online editor at Commentary. She has written for the Weekly Standard, the New York Post and the Washington Examiner. End of article.

This is a full typed copy of the original version of Clinton's letter with addresses included:

July 8, 1971
Berkeley

Dear Saul,

When is that new book coming out - or has it come and I somehow missed the fulfillment of Revelation? I have just had my one-thousandth conversation about <u>Reveille</u> and need some new material to throw at people. You are being rediscovered again as the New Left-type politicos are finally beginning to think seriously about the hard work and mechanics of organizing.

I seem to have survived law school, slightly bruised, with my belief in and zest for organizing intact. If I never thanked you for the encouraging words of last spring in the midst of the Yale-Cambodia madness, I do so now. The more I've seen of places like Yale Law School and the people who haunt them, the more convinced I am that we have the serious business and joy of much work ahead,-- if the commitment to a free and open society is ever going to seem more than eloquence and frustration.

I miss our biennial conversations. Do you ever make it out to California? I am living in Berkeley and working in Oakland for the summer and would love to see you. Let me know if there is any chance of our getting together -- 2667 Derby #2, Berkeley 415-841-5330.

There were rumors of your going to SE Asia to recruit organizers. Is the lack of imagination among my peers really so rampant as that suggests or did you get yourself a CIA-sponsored junket to exotica?

I hope you are still well and fighting. Give my regards to Mrs. Harper. Hopefully we can have a good argument sometime in the near future.

Until then --
Hillary (Signed)

Envelope:
(From)
Hillary Rodham
2667 Derby #2
Berkeley, CA 94705

(To)
MR. SAUL ALINSKY
c/o The Industrial Areas Foundation
8 South Michigan Ave.
Chicago, Illinois

This is another article, from Wikipedia, the free encyclopedia, that gives even more information about Hillary's fascination with the work of Saul Alinsky:

"In 1969, Hillary Rodham wrote a 92-page senior thesis for Wellesley College titled "There Is Only the Fight . . . ": An Analysis of the Alinsky Model. The subject was famed radical community organizer Saul Alinsky.

Contents

1 Thesis
2 White House and Wellesley limiting of access
3 Thesis unveiled
4 References

Thesis:

The thesis offered a critique of Alinsky's methods as largely ineffective, all the while describing Alinsky's personality as appealing. The thesis sought to fit Alinsky into a line of American social activists, including Eugene V. Debs, Martin Luther King, Jr., and Walt Whitman. Written in formal academic language, the thesis concluded that "[Alinsky's] power/conflict model is rendered inapplicable by existing social conflicts" and that Alinsky's model had not expanded nationally due to "the anachronistic nature of small autonomous conflict."

In the acknowledgements and end notes of the thesis, Rodham thanked Alinsky for two interviews and a job offer. She declined the latter, saying that "after spending a year trying to make sense out of [Alinsky's] inconsistency, I need three years of legal rigor." Rodham, an honors student at Wellesley, received an A grade on the thesis.

White House and Wellesley limiting of access:

The work was unnoticed until Hillary Rodham Clinton entered the

White House as First Lady. Clinton researchers and political opponents sought out the thesis, thinking it contained evidence that Rodham had held strong radical or socialist views.

In early 1993, the White House requested that Wellesley not release the thesis to anyone. Wellesley complied, instituting a new rule that closed access to the thesis of any sitting U.S. president or first lady, a rule that in practice applied only to Rodham. Clinton critics and several biographers seized upon this action as a sure sign that the thesis held politically explosive contents that would reveal her radicalism or extremism. Hostile Clinton biographer Barbara Olson wrote in 1999 that Clinton "does not want the American people to know the extent to which she internalized and assimilated the beliefs and methods of Saul Alinsky." In her 2003 memoirs, Clinton mentioned the thesis only briefly, saying she had agreed with some of Alinsky's ideas, but had not agreed with his belief that it was impossible to "change the system" from inside.

Years after the Clintons left the White House, the mystery thesis held its allure; for example, in 2005 Clinton critic Peggy Noonan wrote that it was "the Rosetta Stone of Hillary studies . . . [which] Wellesley College obligingly continues to suppress on her request."

In fact, however, the thesis had been unlocked after the Clintons left the White House in 2001 and is available for reading at the Wellesley College archives. In 2005, msnbc.com investigative reporter Bill Dedman sent his journalism class from Boston University to read the thesis and write articles about it; one of the students, Rick Heller, posted his article online in December 2005. The thesis is also available through interlibrary loan on microfilm, a method reporter Dorian Davis used when he obtained it in January 2007, and sent it to Noonan and to Clinton critic Amanda Carpenter at Human Events, who wrote a piece on it in March. Although publishing the thesis violates copyright, it can nevertheless be found on various websites.

The suppression of the thesis from 1993 to 2001 at the request of the

Clinton White House was documented in March 2007 by reporter Dedman, who read the thesis at the Wellesley library and interviewed Rodham's thesis adviser. Dedman found that the thesis did not disclose Rodham's own views much. A Boston Globe assessment found the thesis nuanced, and said that "While [Rodham] defends Alinsky, she is also dispassionate, disappointed, and amused by his divisive methods and dogmatic ideology." Rodham's former professor and thesis adviser Alan Schechter told msnbc.com that "There Is Only The Fight . . ." was a good thesis, and that its suppression by the Clinton White House "was a stupid political decision, obviously, at the time." End.

Patriotupdate.com has a more current analysis of Hillary Clinton's political positions. This article by David L. Goetsch, on June 30, 2013, is titled: 'Who is worse for America: Barack Obama or Hillary Clinton?'

"When Barack Obama squeaked by Hillary Clinton for the presidential nomination back in 2007, some conservatives sighed in relief and said, "Well at least Hillary won't be president," or words to that effect. Of course, when they made that kind of comment, they knew plenty about Hillary but relatively little about Obama. I wonder if conservatives would make this kind of comment today. The functional question is this: Who is worse for America, Barack Obama or Hillary Clinton? I know what you are thinking. Why not just ask if the reader would rather be run over by a truck or a bus? To paraphrase Hillary Clinton: What does it matter?

The reason I bring up this unwelcome topic is that even with Benghazi on her record and even with her subsequent testimony in which she insulted the grieving families of the Americans who were abandoned and killed in that God-forsaken place, Hillary is still the odds-on favorite to win the Democratic nomination for president. Provided she can stay out of jail over the Benghazi tragedy—and her record of legal slipperiness is well established—the next Republican candidate for the presidency will run against Hillary Clinton. Since this is the case, it behooves all Americans to consider Hillary's beliefs as demonstrated by her own words.

"We are going to take things away from you on behalf of the common good." These may sound like the words of Marx, Lenin, Stalin, or Mao (or Barack Obama for that matter), but they are the words of Hillary Clinton. She made this socialist statement all the way back in 2004, well before Barack Obama introduced the concept of redistribution of wealth as a normal plank in the Democrat's political platform. In other words, Hillary was leaning toward socialism even before Barack Obama took up the cause. Don't forget, before there was Obamacare there was Hillarycare. When it comes to socialized medicine, Obama just finished what Hillary started. (Author's note: Don't forget; the first rule for radicals according to Alinsky is 'Control healthcare and you control the population.)

In 2007, Hillary made it clear that her leftwing philosophy had not changed when she said: "We…can't just let business as usual go on, and that means something has to be taken away from some people." By "business as usual" Hillary meant free market economics in which people pursue opportunity, accept personal responsibility, work hard to build a better life, and enjoy individual and economic freedom. What red-blooded leftist would want this type of business as usual to go on? Not Marx, not Lenin, not Stalin, not Mao, and certainly not Hillary. The "something" that Hillary claimed must be taken away from "some people" is not just money in the form of coercive taxes but freedom—the very freedoms guaranteed in our Constitution.

In the same speech in 2007, Hillary also said: "We have to build a political consensus that requires people to give up a little of their own…in order to create this common ground." Quite a statement. Let's parse her words and see what Hillary really means. She talks about building a "political consensus" but what she really means is a voting majority. In order to pass coercive tax laws that require "people to give up a little of their own," Hillary and her comrades on the left will need a dependable voting majority consisting of people who will be on the receiving end when wealth is redistributed. After all, what sane person is going to willingly give up what he has worked hard to earn when the recipient is someone who not only has not worked hard, but does not intend to. In fact, not only do Hillary's fortunate recipients of other people's money not intend to work, they don't even think they should have to. It's called the entitlement mentality.

Barack Obama ranks right down there among the worst of America's presidents. He is right in there with James Buchanan, Warren Harding, Millard Fillmore, John Tyler, Andrew Johnson, Franklin Pierce, and even Jimmy carter. But even so, I am afraid Hillary will be even worse, provided of course she can win the presidency. It may be hard to imagine things getting worse than they have been under Barack Obama, but I suspect Hillary could manage. End of article.

Discoverthenetworks.org offered an over-all analysis of Hillary Clinton's background and history. These are some important points from that analysis:

1. Rodham was deeply influenced by a 1966 article titled "Change or Containment," which appeared in Motive, a magazine for college-age Methodists. Authored by the Marxist/Maoist theoretician Carl Oglesby, who was a leader of the Students for a Democratic Society, this piece defended Ho Chi Minh, Fidel Castro, and Maoist tactics of violence. Its thesis was that "certain cultural settings" (most notably American capitalism) were inherently inequitable and oppressive, and thus caused people to feel "pain and rage" that sometimes erupted into violence -- like that of "the rioters in Watts or Harlem" -- which was "reactive and provoked" rather than aggressive or malicious. Hillary later said that the Motive article had played a key role in her metamorphosis from Goldwater Republican in 1964 to leftist Democrat in 1968. During her years as First Lady of the United States, Mrs. Clinton would tell a Newsweek reporter that she still treasured the Oglesby piece.

2. Following the June 1968 assassination of Democratic presidential hopeful Robert F. Kennedy, Hillary ended her affiliation with the Wellesley campus Young Republicans and volunteered in New Hampshire to work on the presidential campaign of antiwar candidate Eugene McCarthy. When McCarthy later dropped out of the Democratic primary, Hillary threw her support behind the Party's eventual nominee, Hubert Humphrey. From that point forward, wrote Barbara Olson in her 1999 book Hell to Pay, "Republicans were the enemy and the enemy was allied with evil -- the evils of war, racism, sexism, and poverty."

3. At Yale, Hillary was strongly influenced by the radical theoretician Duncan Kennedy, founder of the academic movement known as critical legal studies, which, drawing on the works of the Frankfurt School, viewed law as a "social construct" that corrupt power structures routinely exploited as an instrument of oppression to protect and promote their own bourgeois values at the expense of the poor and disenfranchised. Advocates of critical legal studies were interested in revolutionary change and the building of a new society founded on Marxist principles.

4. Hillary served as one of nine editors of the Yale Review of Law and Social Action, where she worked collaboratively with Mickey Kantor (who, more than two decades later, would serve as U.S. Trade Representative and U.S. Commerce Secretary under President Bill Clinton) and Robert Reich (who would serve as Bill Clinton's Labor Secretary from 1993 to 1997). "For too long," said the Yale Review, "legal issues have been defined and discussed in terms of academic doctrine rather than strategies for social change." The publication was replete with articles by or about such radicals as William Kunstler, Charles Reich (author of The Greening of America); Jerry Rubin (who wrote a piece exhorting parents to "get high with our seven-year-olds," and urging students to "kill our parents"); and Charles Garry (the civil rights attorney who defended Black Panther Party members accused of murder). The Fall and Winter 1970 editions of the Yale Review, on which Hillary worked as associate editor,

focused heavily on the trials of Black Panthers who had been charged with murder. Numerous cartoons in those issues depicted police officers as hominid pigs.

5. One of Hillary's Yale professors, Thomas Emerson (known as "Tommy the Commie"), introduced her to the aforementioned Charles Garry. Garry helped Hillary get personally involved in the defense of several Black Panthers (including the notorious Bobby Seale) who were then being tried in New Haven, Connecticut for the torture, murder, and mutilation of one of their own members. Though evidence of the defendants' guilt was overwhelming, Hillary -- as part of her coursework for Professor Emerson -- attended the Panther trials and arranged for shifts of fellow students to likewise monitor court proceedings and report on any civil-rights abuses allegedly suffered by the defendants. (Those abuses could then be used, if the Panthers were to lose their case, as grounds for appeal.) Striving to neutralize what she considered the pervasive racism of the American legal system, "Hillary was," as Barbara Olson observed in Hell to Pay, "a budding Leninist."

6. Also in 1972, she went to Berkeley to work as an intern at her hand-picked law firm: Treuhaft, Walker, and Bernstein. Founded by current or former members of the Communist Party USA, this firm had long acted as a legal asset not only for the CPUSA but also for the Black Panthers and other Bay-area radicals. Founding partner Bob Treuhaft, head of the California Communist Party, had been labeled one of the nation's most "dangerously subversive" lawyers. According to historian Stephen Schwartz, "Treuhaft is a man who dedicated his entire legal career to advancing the agenda of the Soviet Communist Party and the KGB." Hillary did yeoman's work while learning at the feet of Treuhaft and his fellow masters. Associates say that Hillary, during her tenure with the firm, helped draftees get themselves declared conscientious objectors so they could avoid serving in Vietnam; they also contend that Hillary served VA interns seeking to avoid taking a loyalty oath to the United States.

7. Edelman went on to help Hillary secure a coveted research position with the Carnegie Council on Children, where the young attorney assisted Yale psychology professor Kenneth Keniston in the production of a report (titled All Our Children) advocating a dramatic expansion of social-welfare entitlements and a national guaranteed income -- all in the name of children's rights. Moreover, the report maintained that the traditional nuclear family was not inherently preferable to any other family structure, and that society had an obligation to honor, encourage, and support alternate arrangements such as single-parent households. What really mattered, said the Council, was the network of professionals -- teachers, pediatricians, social workers, and day-care workers -- who would collectively play the most vital role in raising children properly. In short, the Carnegie Council preached that childrearing was less a parental matter than a societal task to be overseen by "public advocates" -- judges, bureaucrats, social workers and other "experts" in childrearing -- who could intervene between parents and children on the latter's behalf. According to the report, the role of parents should be subordinate to the role of these experts.

8. Viewing America as an authoritarian, patriarchal, male-dominated society that tended to oppress women, children, and minorities, Hillary wrote a November 1973 article for the Harvard Educational Review advocating the liberation of children from "the empire of the father." She claimed that the traditional nuclear family structure often undermined the best interests of children, who "consequently need social institutions specifically designed to safeguard their position." "Along with the family," she elaborated, "past and present examples of such arrangements include marriage, slavery, and the Indian Reservation system." She added: "Decisions about motherhood and abortion, schooling, cosmetic surgery, treatment of venereal disease, or employment, and others where the decision or lack of one will significantly affect a child's future should not be made unilaterally by parents."

9. Decades later, Hillary would take up these themes again in her

1996 book It Takes a Village, which stressed the importance of the larger community of adults -- many of whom are paid caretakers whose labors are funded by American taxpayers -- in childrearing.

10. Bill Clinton served as Governor of Arkansas from 1978 to 1980, and again from 1982 to 1992. Thus Mrs. Clinton spent a total of twelve years as Arkansas's First Lady. During that time, she continued her legal practice as a partner in the Rose Law Firm. In 1978 she became a board member of the Children's Defense Fund (CDF), and from 1986 to 1992 she served as chair of the CDF Board. From 1982 to 1988 Mrs. Clinton also chaired the New World Foundation (NWF), which had helped to launch CDF in 1973. During her years at NWF's helm, the Foundation made grants to such organizations as the National Lawyers Guild, the Institute for Policy Studies, the Christic Institute, Grassroots International, the Committees in Solidarity with the People of El Salvador (which sought to foment a Communist revolution in Central America), and groups with ties to the most extreme elements of the African National Congress.

11. In the spring of 1993, shortly after her husband took his oath of office, Mrs. Clinton delivered the commencement address at the University of Texas. In her speech, she stated: "We are at a stage in history in which remolding society is one of the great challenges facing all of us in the West."

12. That same year, Mrs. Clinton latched onto the phrase "the politics of meaning," an opaque concept coined by Michael Lerner that blended radical politics with New Ageish human potentialism. She invited Lerner to the White House, briefly making him her "guru" until the ridicule which this caused made her retreat from the connection. (In her autobiography, Mrs. Clinton strenuously avoids any mention of Lerner, or of Lerner's Tikkun magazine.)

13. Also during her early years as First Lady, Mrs. Clinton was put in charge of the 500-member Health Care Task Force which tried, in secret meetings and by stealth, to socialize medical care in the United

States, a sector that represented approximately one-seventh of the U.S. economy. This modus operandi was in violation of so-called "sunshine laws," which forbid such secret meetings from taking place when non-government employees are present. Mrs. Clinton was sued by the Association of American Physicians and Surgeons for these violations. The trial judge, U.S. District Judge Royce C. Lamberth, ultimately ruled against her and the Clinton administration. In December 1997 Lamberth issued a 19-page report condemning as "reprehensible" the duplicity exhibited by Mrs. Clinton's Task Force. "The Executive Branch of the government, working in tandem, was dishonest with this court, and the government must now face the consequences of its misconduct," said Lamberth. "It is clear," he added, "that the decisions here were made at the highest levels of government. There were no rogue lawyers here misleading the court."

The linchpin of Mrs. Clinton's healthcare plan was a mandate forcing all Americans to purchase insurance, and imposing a penalty on those who failed to comply. In November 2013, MIT professor John Gruber, who was a chief architect of the Patient Protection & Affordable Care Act (Obamacare), said that Hillary Clinton's 1990s-era plan was "much more interventionist" than Obamacare, "much to the left of Obamacare," and "would have more radically changed our healthcare system."

14. During the 1990s, Mrs. Clinton spent eight years faithfully attending Foundry United Methodist Church in Washington, D.C., which was then pastored by the Rev. Dr. J. Philip Wogaman. Wogaman had made his political worldview clear in his many writings and sermons over the years. For instance, in 1990, a year after the fall of the Berlin Wall, he wrote that "Christian socialism's critique of the excesses and brutalities and idolatries of the free market still need to be heard." On an earlier occasion, he had lauded the "modest but real economic success" of Communist Cuba and China. As long ago as 1967, Wogaman had written: "The USSR is characteristic of the more tolerant Communist arrangements for religion. In Russia there are specific constitutional guarantees of

freedom of worship, and some provision has even been made for the upkeep of churches and theological seminaries."

By no means was Wogaman the only radical cleric to be admired by Mrs. Clinton. In her 2004 memoir, Living History, Mrs. Clinton praised Rev. William Sloane Coffin Jr., who had served as Yale's chaplain during Hillary's years at the law school, for his "articulate moral critique of American involvement" in Vietnam. That critique involved his traveling to Hanoi in 1972. Seven years later, he would make a friendly trip to Tehran, capital of the first modern Islamic theocratic state which had just stormed a U.S. embassy and kidnapped dozens of his fellow countrymen.

15. Hillary's Nasty, Disrespectful Treatment of Secret Service & Military Personnel: In his 2014 book The First Family Detail, bestselling author Ronald Kessler writes that during Mrs. Clinton's years as First Lady, she was known and despised by Secret Service agents and military personnel for the nasty treatment, explosive temper, and imperious attitude she conveyed toward them. "Agents say being on Hillary Clinton's detail is the worst duty assignment in the Secret Service," writes Kessler. "Being assigned to her detail is a form of punishment." In August 2014, the Daily Mail provided the following details from Kessler's book:

"'We were basically told, the Clintons don't want to see you, they don't want to hear you, get of the way,' according to a former Secret Service agent."

"She didn't like law enforcement officers or the military, former Secret Service agent Lloyd Bulman stated. 'She was just really rude to almost everybody. She'd act like she didn't want you around, like you were beneath her.' She went years without speaking to some agents."

"In response to a cheerful 'Good morning, ma'am,' by a former uniformed officer, Hillary's response to him was 'F--k off.'"

"While publicly courting law enforcement organizations, privately she felt disdain. She wanted state troopers and local police to wear suits and drive unmarked cars. No military aides could wear their uniforms in the White House. If agents driving her went over a bump, she'd swear at them."

"Glad-handing on the road on her Senatorial campaign, when they arrived at a 4-F Club in the land of dairy cows in upstate New York, she saw cows and people in jeans. That enraged her and she asked a staffer, 'What the f*** did we come her for? There's no money here.'"

"White House deputy counsel Vince Foster, who committed suicide in June 1993, was on the receiving end of a virulent verbal attack by Hillary. She disagreed with a legal opinion he made and humiliated him in a meeting, stating he would never be more than a hick-town lawyer and wasn't ready for the big time. 'The put-down that she gave him in that big meeting just pushed him over the edge', [former FBI agent Coy] Copeland says. She blamed Foster for all of the Clinton's problems and stated he had failed the couple...."

16. Analysis of Hillary's Worldview and Agendas:

"Hillary Clinton's alliances with organizations like CAP, MMFA, and ACS serve as indicators of her most deeply held political beliefs and objectives. David Horowitz has provided the following incisive analysis of Mrs. Clinton's broad agendas and the tactics she employs in pursuit of them:

"It is possible to be a socialist, and radical in one's agendas, and yet moderate in the means one regards as practical to achieve them. To change the world, it is first necessary to acquire cultural and political power. And these transitional goals may often be accomplished by indirection and deception even more effectively than by frontal assault. ... New Left progressives [such as] Hillary Clinton ... [share the] intoxicating vision of a social redemption achieved by Them ...

For these self-appointed social redeemers, the goal -- 'social justice' -- is not about rectifying particular injustices, which would be practical and modest, and therefore conservative. Their crusade is about rectifying injustice in the very order of things. 'Social Justice' for them is about a world reborn, a world in which prejudice and violence are absent, in which everyone is equal and equally advantaged and without fundamentally conflicting desires. It is a world that could only come into being through a re-structuring of human nature and of society itself. ... In other words, a world in which human consciousness is changed, human relations refashioned, social institutions transformed, and in which 'social justice' prevails. ... In short, the transformation of the world requires the permanent entrenchment of the saints in power. Therefore, everything is justified that serves to achieve the continuance of Them. ... The focus of Hillary Clinton's ambition ... is the vision of a world that can only be achieved when the Chosen accumulate enough power to change this one." End of discoverthenetworks article.

Attachment 2
The Third Jihad

This article reveals the Third Jihad planned and executed by the Muslim Brotherhood. This is from Discoverthenetworks.org:

http://www.discoverthenetworks.org/viewSubCategory.asp?id=1235

"In July 2007, seven key leaders of an Islamic charity known as the Holy Land Foundation for Relief and Development (HLF) went on trial for charges that they had: (a) provided "material support and resources" to a foreign terrorist organization (namely Hamas); (b) engaged in money laundering; and (c) breached the International Emergency Economic Powers Act, which prohibits transactions that threaten American national security. Along with the seven named defendants, the U.S. government released a list of approximately 300 "unindicted co-conspirators" and "joint venturers." During the course of the HLF trial, many incriminating documents were entered into evidence. Perhaps the most significant of these was "An Explanatory Memorandum on the General Strategic Goal for the Group in North America," by the Muslim Brotherhood operative Mohamed Akram. Federal investigators found Akram's memo in the home of Ismael Elbarasse, a founder of the Dar Al-Hijrah mosque in Falls Church, Virginia, during a 2004 search. Elbarasse was a member of the Palestine Committee, which the Muslim Brotherhood had created to support Hamas in the United States.

Written sometime in 1987 but not formally published until May 22, 1991, Akram's 18-page document listed the Brotherhood's 29 likeminded "organizations of our friends" that shared the common goal of dismantling American institutions and turning the U.S. into a Muslim nation. These "friends" were identified by Akram and the Brotherhood as groups that could help convince Muslims "that their work in America is a kind of grand Jihad in eliminating and destroying the Western civilization from within and 'sabotaging' its miserable house by their hands ... so that ... God's religion [Islam] is made victorious over all other religions."

Akram was well aware that in the U.S., it would be extremely difficult to promote Islam by means of terror attacks. Thus the "grand jihad" that he and his Brotherhood comrades envisioned was not a violent one involving bombings and shootings, but rather a stealth (or "soft") jihad aiming to impose Islamic law (Sharia) over every region of the earth by incremental, non-confrontational means, such as working to "expand the observant Muslim base"; to "unif[y] and direc[t] Muslims' efforts"; and to "present Islam as a civilization alternative." At its heart, Akram's document details a plan to conquer and Islamize the United States – not as an ultimate objective, but merely as a stepping stone toward the larger goal of one day creating "the global Islamic state."

In line with this objective, Akram and the Brotherhood resolved to "settle" Islam and the Islamic movement within the United States, so that the Muslim religion could be "enabled within the souls, minds and the lives of the people of the country." Akram explained that this could be accomplished "through the establishment of firmly-rooted organizations on whose bases civilization, structure and testimony are built." He urged Muslim leaders to make "a shift from the collision mentality to the absorption mentality," meaning that they should abandon any tactics involving defiance or confrontation, and seek instead to implant into the larger society a host of seemingly benign Islamic groups with ostensibly unobjectionable motives; once those groups had gained a measure of public acceptance, they would be in a position to more effectively promote societal transformation by the old Communist technique of "boring from within."

"The heart and the core" of this strategy, said Akram, was contingent upon these groups' ability to develop "a mastery of the art of 'coalitions.'" That is, by working synergistically they could complement, augment, and amplify one another's efforts. Added Akram: "The big challenge that is ahead of us is how to turn these seeds or 'scattered' elements into comprehensive, stable, 'settled' organizations that are connected with our Movement and which fly in our orbit and take orders from our guidance." The ultimate objective was not only an enlarged Muslim presence, but also implementation of the Brotherhood objectives of transforming pluralistic societies, particularly America, into Islamic states, and sweeping away Western notions of legal equality, freedom of conscience, freedom of religion, and freedom of speech.

Akram and the Brotherhood understood that in order to succeed in this endeavor, they needed to appeal to different strata of the American population in different ways; that whereas some people could be influenced by messages delivered from a religious perspective, others would be more responsive to messages delivered by educators, or bankers, or political figures, or journalists, etc. Thus, Akram's blueprint for the advancement of the Islamic movement stressed the need to form a coalition of groups coming from the worlds of education; religious proselytization; political activism; audio and video production; print media; banking and finance; the physical sciences; the social sciences; professional and business networking; cultural affairs; the publishing and distribution of books; children and teenagers; women's rights; vocational concerns; and jurisprudence.

By promoting the Islamic movement on such a wide variety of fronts, the Brotherhood and its allies could multiply exponentially their influence. Toward that end, the Akram/Brotherhood "Explanatory Memorandum" named the following 29 groups as the organizations they believed could collaborate effectively to destroy America from within – "if they all march according to one plan":

In the name of God, the Beneficent, the Merciful Thanks be to God, Lord of the Two Worlds, Prayers and peace be upon the master of the Messengers.

An Explanatory Memorandum
On the General Strategic Goal for the Group In North America 5/22/1991

Contents:

1- An introduction in explanation
2- The Concept of Settlement
3- The Process of Settlement
4- Comprehensive Settlement Organizations

In the name of God, the Beneficent, the Merciful Thanks be to God, Lord of the Two Worlds And Blessed are the Pious

The beloved brother/The General Masul, may God keep him
The beloved brother/Secretary of the Shura Council, may God keep him
The beloved brothers/Members of the Shura Council, may God keep them
God's peace, mercy and blessings be upon you.... To proceed,

I ask Almighty God that you, your families and those whom you love around you are in the best of conditions, pleasing to God, glorified His name be.

I send this letter of mine to you hoping that it would seize your attention and receive your good care as you are the people of responsibility and those to whom trust is given. Between your hands is an "Explanatory Memorandum" which I put effort in writing down so that it is not locked in the chest and the mind, and so that I can share with you a portion of the responsibility in leading the Group in this country.

What might have encouraged me to submit the memorandum in this time in particular is my feeling of a "glimpse of hope" and the beginning of good tidings which bring the good news that we have embarked on a new stage of Islamic activism stages in this continent. The papers which are between your hands are not abundant extravagance, imaginations or hallucinations which passed in the mind of one of your brothers, but they are rather hopes, ambitions and challenges that I hope that you share some or most of which with me. I do not claim their infallibility or absolute correctness, but they are an attempt which requires study, outlook, detailing and rooting from you.

My request to my brothers is to read the memorandum and to write what they wanted of comments and corrections, keeping in mind that what is between your hands is not strange or a new submission without a root, but rather an attempt to interpret and explain some of what came in the long-term plan which we approved and adopted in our council and our conference in the year (1987).

So, my honorable brother, do not rush to throw these papers away due to your many occupations and worries. All what I'm asking of you is to read them and to comment on them hoping that we might continue together the project of our plan and our Islamic work in this part of the world. Should you do that, I would be thankful and grateful to you.

I also ask my honorable brother, the Secretary of the Council, to add the subject of the memorandum on the Council agenda in its coming meeting.

May God reward you good and keep you for His Daw'a
Your brother/Mohamed Akram

In the name of God, the Beneficent, the Merciful Thanks be to God, Lord of the Two Worlds And Blessed are the Pious

Subject: A project for an explanatory memorandum for the General Strategic goal for the Group in North America mentioned in the long-term plan

One: The Memorandum is derived from:

1- The general strategic goal of the Group in America which was approved by the Shura Council and the Organizational Conference for the year [1987] is "Enablement of Islam in North America, meaning: establishing an effective and a stable Islamic Movement led by the Muslim Brotherhood which adopts Muslims' causes domestically and globally, and which works to expand the observant Muslim base, aims at unifying and directing Muslims' efforts, presents Islam as a civilization alternative, and supports the global Islamic State wherever it is".

2- The priority that is approved by the Shura Council for the work of the Group in its current and former session which is "Settlement".

3- The positive development with the brothers in the Islamic Circle in an attempt to reach a unity of merger.

4- The constant need for thinking and future planning, an attempt to read it and working to "shape" the present to comply and suit the needs and challenges of the future.

5- The paper of his eminence, the General Masul, may God keep him, which he recently sent to the members of the Council.

Two: An Introduction to the Explanatory Memorandum:

In order to begin with the explanation, we must "summon" the following question and place it in front of our eyes as its relationship is important and necessary with the strategic goal and the explanation project we are embarking on. The question we are facing is: "How do you like to see the Islam Movement in North America in ten years?", or "taking along" the following sentence when planning and working, "Islamic Work in North America in the year (2000): A Strategic Vision".

Also, we must summon and take along "elements" of the general strategic goal of the Group in North America and I will intentionally repeat them in numbers. They are:

1-Establishing an effective and stable Islamic Movement led by the Muslim Brotherhood.
2- Adopting Muslims' causes domestically and globally.
3- Expanding the observant Muslim base.
4- Unifying and directing Muslims' effort
5- Presenting Islam as a civilization alternative
6- Supporting the establishment of the global Islamic State wherever it is.

It must be stressed that it has become clear and emphatically known that all is in agreement that we must "settle" or "enable" Islam and its Movement in this part of the world. Therefore, a joint understanding of the meaning of settlement or enablement must be adopted, through which and on whose basis we explain the general strategic goal with its six elements for the Group in North America.

Three: The Concept of Settlement:

This term was mentioned in the Group's "dictionary" and documents with various meanings in spite of the fact that everyone meant one thing with it. We believe that the understanding of the essence is the same and we will attempt here to give the word and its "meanings" a practical explanation with a practical Movement tone, and not a philosophical linguistic explanation, while stressing that this explanation of ours is not complete until our explanation of "the process" of settlement itself is understood which is mentioned in the following paragraph. We briefly say the following:

Settlement: "That Islam and its Movement become a part of the homeland it lives in". Establishment: "That Islam turns into firmly-rooted organizations on whose bases civilization, structure and testimony are built". Stability: "That Islam is stable in the land on which its people move". Enablement: "That Islam is enabled within the souls, minds and the lives of the people of the country in which it moves". Rooting: "That Islam is resident and not a passing thing, or rooted "entrenched" in the soil of the spot where it moves and not a strange plant to it".

Four: The Process of Settlement:

In order for Islam and its Movement to become "a part of the homeland" in which it lives, "stable" in its land, "rooted" in the spirits and minds of its people, "enabled" in the live of its society and has firmly-established "organizations" on which the Islamic structure is built and with which the testimony of civilization is achieved, the Movement must plan and struggle to obtain "the keys" and the tools of this process in carry out this grand mission as a "Civilization Jihadist" responsibility which lies on the shoulders of Muslims and - on top of them - the Muslim Brotherhood in this country. Among these keys and tools are the following:

1- Adopting the concept of settlement and understanding its practical meanings:

The Explanatory Memorandum focused on the Movement and the realistic dimension of the process of settlement and its practical meanings without paying attention to the difference in understanding between the resident and the non-resident, or who is the settled and the non-settled and we believe that what was mentioned in the long-term plan in that regards suffices.

2- Making a fundamental shift in our thinking and mentality in order to suit the challenges of the settlement mission.

What is meant with the shift - which is a positive expression - is responding to the grand challenges of the settlement issues. We believe that any transforming response begins with the method of thinking and its center, the brain, first. In order to clarify what is meant with the shift as a key to qualify us to enter the field of settlement, we say very briefly that the following must be accomplished:

A shift from the partial thinking mentality to the comprehensive thinking mentality.

A shift from the "amputated" partial thinking mentality to the "continuous" comprehensive mentality.

A shift from the mentality of caution and reservation to the mentality of risk and controlled liberation.

A shift from the mentality of the elite Movement to the mentality of the popular Movement.

A shift from the mentality of preaching and guidance to the mentality of building and testimony

A shift from the single opinion mentality to the multiple opinion mentality.

A shift from the collision mentality to the absorption mentality.

A shift from the individual mentality to the team mentality.

A shift from the anticipation mentality to the initiative mentality.

A shift from the hesitation mentality to the decisiveness mentality.

A shift from the principles mentality to the programs mentality.

A shift from the abstract ideas mentality the true organizations mentality [This is the core point and the essence of the memorandum].

3- Understanding the historical stages in which the Islamic Ikhwani activism went through in this country:

The writer of the memorandum believes that understanding and comprehending the historical stages of the Islamic activism which was led and being led by the Muslim Brotherhood in this continent is a very important key in working towards settlement, through which the Group observes its march, the direction of its movement and the curves and turns of its road. We will suffice here with mentioning the title for each of these stages [The title expresses the prevalent characteristic of the stage] [Details maybe mentioned in another future study]. Most likely, the stages are:

A- The stage of searching for self and determining the identity.

B- The stage of inner build-up and tightening the organization.

C- The stage of mosques and the Islamic centers.

D- The stage of building the Islamic organizations - the first phase.

E- The stage of building the Islamic schools - the first phase.

F- The stage of thinking about the overt Islamic Movement - the first phase.

G- The stage of openness to the other Islamic movements and attempting to reach a formula for dealing with them - the first phase.

H- The stage of reviving and establishing the Islamic organizations - the second phase.

We believe that the Group is embarking on this stage in its second phase as it has to open the door and enter as it did the first time.

4-Understanding the role of the Muslim Brother in North America:

The process of settlement is a "Civilization-Jihadist Process" with all the word means. The Ikhwan must understand that their work in America is a kind of grand Jihad in eliminating and destroying the Western civilization from within and "sabotaging" its miserable house by their hands and the hands of the believers so that it is eliminated and God's religion is made victorious over all other religions. Without this level of understanding, we are not up to this challenge and have not prepared ourselves for Jihad yet. It is a Muslim's destiny to perform Jihad and work wherever he is and wherever he lands until the final hour comes, and there is no escape from that destiny except for those who chose to slack. But, would the slackers and the Mujahedeen be equal.

5-Understanding that we cannot perform the settlement mission by ourselves or away from people:

A mission as significant and as huge as the settlement mission needs magnificent and exhausting efforts. With their capabilities, human, financial and scientific resources, the Ikhwan will not be able to carry out this mission alone or away from people and he who believes that is wrong, and God knows best. As for the role of the Ikhwan, it is the initiative, pioneering, leadership, raising the banner and pushing people in that direction. They are then to work to employ, direct and unify Muslims' efforts and powers for this process. In order to do that, we must possess a mastery of the art of "coalitions", the art of "absorption" and the principles of "cooperation".

6-The necessity of achieving a union and balanced gradual merger between private work and public work:
We believe that what was written about this subject is many and is enough. But, it needs a time and a practical frame so that what is needed is achieved in a gradual and a balanced way that is compatible with the process of settlement.

7-The conviction that the success of the settlement of Islam and its Movement in this country is a success to the global Islamic Movement and a true support for the sought-after state, God willing:
There is a conviction - with which this memorandum disagrees - that our focus in attempting to settle Islam in this country will lead to negligence in our duty towards the global Islamic Movement in supporting its project to establish the state. We believe that the reply is in two segments: One - The success of the Movement in America in establishing an observant Islamic base with power and effectiveness will be the best support and aid to the global Movement project. And the second - is the global Movement has not succeeded yet in "distributing roles" to its branches, stating what is the needed from them as one of the participants or contributors to the project to establish the global Islamic state. The day this happens, the children of the American Ikhwani branch will have far-reaching impact and positions that make the ancestors proud.

8-Absorbing Muslims and winning them with all of their factions and colors in America and Canada for the settlement project, and making it their cause, future and the basis of their Islamic life in this part of the world:

This issues requires from us to learn "the art of dealing with the others", as people are different and people in many colors. We need to adopt the principle which says, "Take from people... the best they have", their best specializations, experiences, arts, energies and abilities. By people here we mean those within or without the ranks of individuals and organizations. The policy of "taking" should be with what achieves the strategic goal and the settlement process. But the big challenge in front of us is: how to connect them all in "the orbit" of our plan and "the circle" of our Movement in order to achieve "the core" of our interest. To me, there is no choice for us other than alliance and mutual understanding of those who desire from our religion and those who agree from our belief in work. And the U.S. Islamic arena is full of those waiting...., the pioneers.

What matters is bringing people to the level of comprehension of the challenge that is facing us as Muslims in this country, conviction of our settlement project, and understanding the benefit of agreement, cooperation and alliance. At that time, if we ask for money, a lot of it would come, and if we ask for men, they would come in lines. What matters is that our plan is "the criterion and the balance" in our relationship with others.

Here, two points must be noted; the first one: we need to comprehend and understand the balance of the Islamic powers in the U.S. arena [and this might be the subject of a future study]. The second point: what we reached with the brothers in "ICNA" is considered a step in the right direction, the beginning of good and the first drop that requires growing and guidance.

9-Re-examining our organizational and administrative bodies, the type of leadership and the method of selecting it with what suits the challenges of the settlement mission:

The memorandum will be silent about details regarding this item even though it is logical and there is a lot to be said about it,

10-Growing and developing our resources and capabilities, our financial and human resources with what suits the magnitude of the grand mission:

If we examined the human and the financial resources the Ikhwan alone own in this country, we and others would feel proud and glorious. And if we add to them the resources of our friends and allies, those who circle in our orbit and those waiting on our banner, we would realize that we are able to open the door to settlement and walk through it seeking to make Almighty God's word the highest.

11-Utilizing the scientific method in planning, thinking and preparation of studies needed for the process of settlement:

Yes, we need this method, and we need many studies which aid in this civilization Jihadist operation. We will mention some of them briefly:

The history of the Islamic presence in America.

The history of the Islamic Ikhwani presence in America.

Islamic movements, organizations and organizations: analysis and criticism.

The phenomenon of the Islamic centers and schools: challenges, needs and statistics.

Islamic minorities,

Muslim and Arab communities.

The U.S. society: make-up and politics.

The U.S. society's view of Islam and Muslims... And many other studies which we can direct our brothers and allies to prepare, either through their academic studies or through their educational centers or organizational tasking. What is important is that we start.

12-Agreeing on a flexible, balanced and a clear "mechanism" to implement the process of settlement within a specific, gradual and balanced "time frame" that is in-line with the demands and challenges of the process of settlement.

13-Understanding the U.S. society from its different aspects an understanding that "qualifies" us to perform the mission of settling our Dawa' in its country "and growing it" on its land.

14-Adopting a written "jurisprudence" that includes legal and movement bases, principles, policies and interpretations which are suitable for the needs and challenges of the process of settlement.

15-Agreeing on "criteria" and balances to be a sort of "antennas" or "the watch tower" in order to make sure that all of our priorities, plans, programs, bodies, leadership, monies and activities march towards the process of the settlement.

16-Adopting a practical, flexible formula through which our central work complements our domestic work.

17-Understanding the role and the nature of work of "The Islamic Center" in every city with what achieves the goal of the process of settlement:
The center we seek is the one which constitutes the "axis" of our Movement, the "perimeter" of the circle of our work, our "balance center", the "base" for our rise and our "Dar al-Arqam" to educate us, prepare us and supply our battalions in addition to being the "niche" of our prayers.

This is in order for the Islamic center to turn - in action not in words - into a seed "for a small Islamic society" which is a reflection and a mirror to our central organizations. The center ought to turn into a "beehive" which produces sweet honey. Thus, the Islamic center would turn into a place for study, family, battalion, course, seminar, visit, sport, school, social club, women gathering, kindergarten for male and female youngsters, the office of the domestic political resolution, and the center for distributing our newspapers, magazines, books and our audio and visual tapes.

In brief we say: we would like for the Islamic center to become "The House of Dawa'" and "the general center" in deeds first before name. As much as we own and direct these centers at the continent level, we can say we are marching successfully towards the settlement of Dawa' in this country.

Meaning that the "center's" role should be the same as the "mosque's" role during the time of God's prophet, God's prayers and peace be upon him, when he marched to "settle" the Dawa' in its first generation in Madina. from the mosque, he drew the Islamic life and provided to the world the most magnificent and fabulous civilization humanity knew.

This mandates that, eventually, the region, the branch and the Usra turn into "operations rooms" for planning, direction, monitoring and leadership for the Islamic center in order to be a role model to be followed.

18-Adopting a system that is based on "selecting" workers, "role distribution" and "assigning" positions and responsibilities is based on specialization, desire and need with what achieves the process of settlement and contributes to its success.

19-Turning the principle of dedication for the Masuls of main positions within the Group into a rule, a basis and a policy in work. Without it, the process of settlement might be stalled [Talking about this point requires more details and discussion].

20-Understanding the importance of the "Organizational" shift in our Movement work, and doing Jihad in order to achieve it in the real world with what serves the process of settlement and expedites its results, God Almighty's willing:

The reason this paragraph was delayed is to stress its utmost importance as it constitutes the heart and the core of this memorandum. It also constitutes the practical aspect and the true measure of our success or failure in our march towards settlement. The talk about the organizations and the "organizational" mentality or phenomenon does not require much details. It suffices to say that the first pioneer of this phenomenon was our prophet Mohamed, God's peace, mercy and blessings be upon him, as he placed the foundation for the first civilized organization which is the mosque, which truly became "the comprehensive organization". And this was done by the pioneer of the contemporary Islamic Dawa', Imam martyr Hasan al-Banna, may God have mercy on him, when he and his brothers felt the need to "re-establish" Islam and its movement anew, leading him to establish organizations with all their kinds: economic, social, media, scouting, professional and even the military ones. We must say that we are in a country which understands no language other than the language of the organizations, and one which does not respect or give weight to any group without effective, functional and strong organizations.

It is good fortune that there are brothers among us who have this "trend", mentality or inclination to build the organizations who have beat us by action and words which leads us to dare say honestly what Sadat in Egypt once said, "We want to build a country of organizations" - a word of right he meant wrong with. I say to my brothers, let us raise the banner of truth to establish right "We want to establish the Group of organizations", as without it we will not able to put our feet on the true path.

And in order for the process of settlement to be completed, we must plan and work from now to equip and prepare ourselves, our brothers, our apparatuses, our sections and our committees in order to turn into comprehensive organizations in a gradual and balanced way that is suitable with the need and the reality. What encourages us to do that - in addition to the aforementioned -is that we possess "seeds" for each organization from the organization we call for [See attachment number (1)]. All we need is to tweak them, coordinate their work, collect their elements and merge their efforts with others and then connect them with the comprehensive plan we seek.

For instance, We have a seed for a "comprehensive media and art" organization: we own a print + advanced typesetting machine + audio and visual center + art production office + magazines in Arabic and English [The Horizons, The Hope, The Politicians, Ha Falastine, Press Clips, al-Zaytouna, Palestine Monitor, Social Sciences Magazines...] + art band + photographers + producers + programs anchors + journalists + in addition to other media and art experiences". Another example:

We have a seed for a "comprehensive Dawa' educational" organization: We have the Daw'a section in ISNA + Dr. Jamal Badawi Foundation + the center run by brother Hamed al-Ghazali + the Dawa' center the Dawa' Committee and brother Shaker al-Sayyed are seeking to establish now + in addition to other Daw'a efforts here and there...". And this applies to all the organizations we call on establishing.

The big challenge that is ahead of us is how to turn these seeds or "scattered" elements into comprehensive, stable, "settled" organizations that are connected with our Movement and which fly in our orbit and take orders from our guidance. This does not prevent - but calls for - each central organization to have its local branches but its connection with the Islamic center in the city is a must.

What is needed is to seek to prepare the atmosphere and the means to achieve "the merger" so that the sections, the committees, the regions, the branches and the Usras are eventually the heart and the core of these organizations.

Or, for the shift and the change to occur as follows:

1- The Movement Department + The Secretariat Department
2- Education Department + Dawa'a Com.
3- Sisters Department
4- The Financial Department + Investment Committee + The Endowment
5- Youth Department + Youths Organizations Department
6- The Social Committee + Matrimony Committee + Mercy Foundation
7- The Security Committee
8- The Political Depart. + Palestine Com.
9- The Group's Court + The Legal Com.
10-Domestic Work Department
11-Our magazines + the print + our art band
12-The Studies Association + The Publication House + Dar al-Kitab
13-Scientific and Medial societies
14-The Organizational Conference
15-The Shura Council + Planning Com.
16-The Executive Office
17-The General Masul

The **Organizational & Administrative Organization**

The General Center
Dawa' and Educational Organization
The Women's Organization
The Economic Organization
Youth Organizations
The Social Organization
The Security Organization
The Political Organization
The Judicial Organization
Its work is to be distributed to the rest of the organizations
The Media and Art Organization
The Intellectual & Cultural Organization
Scientific, Educational & Professional Organization
The Islamic-American Founding Conference
The Shura Council for the Islamic-American Movement
The Executive Office of the Islamic-American Movement
Chairman of the Islamic Movement and its official Spokesman
Field leaders of organizations & Islamic centers

Five: Comprehensive Settlement Organization:

We would then seek and struggle in order to make each one of these above-mentioned organizations a "comprehensive organization" throughout the days and the years, and as long as we are destined to be in this country. What is important is that we put the foundation and we will be followed by peoples and generations that would finish the march and the road but with a clearly-defined guidance.

And, in order for us to clarify what we mean with the comprehensive, specialized organization, we mention here the characteristics and traits of each organization of the "promising" organizations.

1-From the Dawa' and educational aspect [The Dawa* and Educational Organization]: to include:

The Organization to spread the Dawa' (Central and local branches).
An institute to graduate Callers and Educators.
Scholars, Callers, Educators, Preachers and Program Anchors.
Art and communication technology, Conveyance and Dawa'.
A television station.
A specialized Dawa' magazine.
A radio station.
The Higher Islamic Council for Callers and Educators.
The Higher Council for Mosques and Islamic Centers.
Friendship Societies with the other religions... and things like that.

2-Politically [The Political Organization]: to include:

A central political party.
Local political offices.
Political symbols.
Relationships and alliances.
The American Organization for Islamic Political Action
Advanced Information Centers....and things like that.

3-Media [The Media and Art Organization]: to include:

A daily newspaper,
Weekly, monthly and seasonal magazines.
Radio stations.

Television programs.

Audio and visual centers.

A magazine for the Muslim child.

A magazine for the Muslim woman.

A print and typesetting machines.

A production office.

A photography and recording studio

Art bands for acting, chanting and theater.

A marketing and art production office... and things like that.

4-Economically [The Economic Organization!: to include:An Islamic Central bank.

Islamic endowments.

Investment projects.

An organization for interest-free loans.... and things like that.

5-Scientifically and Professionally [The Scientific. Educational and Professional Organization]: to include:

Scientific research centers.

Technical organizations and vocational training.

An Islamic university.

Islamic schools.

A council for education and scientific research.

Centers to train teachers.

Scientific societies in schools.

An office for academic guidance.

A body for authorship and Islamic curricula.... and things like that.

6-Culturally and Intellectually [The Cultural and Intellectual Organization]: to include:

A center for studies and research.

Cultural and intellectual foundations such as [The Social Scientists Society - Scientists and Engineers Society....].
An organization for Islamic thought and culture.
A publication, translation and distribution house for Islamic books.
An office for archiving, history and authentication
The project to translate the Noble Quran, the Noble Sayings....and things like that.

7-Socially [The Social-Charitable Organization]: to include:

Social clubs for the youths and the community's sons and daughters
Local societies for social welfare and the services are tied to the Islamic centers
The Islamic Organization to Combat the Social Ills of the U.S. Society
Islamic houses project
Matrimony and family cases office....and things like that.

8-Youths [The Youth Organization!: to include:
Central and local youths foundations.
Sports teams and clubs
Scouting teams....and things like that.

9-Women [The Women Organization]: to include:

Central and local women societies.
Organizations of training, vocational and housekeeping.
An organization to train female preachers.
Islamic kindergartens...and things like that.

10-Organizationally and Administratively [The Administrative and Organizational Organization!: to include:

An institute for training, growth, development and planning
Prominent experts in this field
Work systems, bylaws and charters fit for running the most complicated bodies and organizations
A periodic magazine in Islamic development and administration.
Owning camps and halls for the various activities.
A data, polling and census bank.
An advanced communication network.
An advanced archive for our heritage and production....and things like that.

11-Security [The Security Organization!: to include:

Clubs for training and learning self-defense techniques.
A center which is concerned with the security issues [Technical, intellectual, technological and human]....and things like that.

12-Legally [The Legal Organization]: to include:

A Central Jurisprudence Council.
A Central Islamic Court.
Muslim Attorneys Society.
The Islamic Foundation for Defense of Muslims' Rights...and things like that. And success is by God.

A list of our organizations and the organizations of our friends [Imagine if they all march according to one plan!!!]

ISNA – Islamic Society of North America
MSA – Muslim Students Association
MCA – The Muslim Communities Association
AMSS – The Association of Muslim Social Scientists
AMSE – The Association of Muslim Scientists and Engineers
IMA – Islamic Medical Association
ITC – Islamic Teaching Center
NAIT – North American Islamic Trust
FID – Foundation for International Development
IHC – Islamic Housing Cooperative
ICD – Islamic Centers Division
ATP – American Trust Publishers
AVC – Audio-Visual Center
IBS – Islamic Book Service
MBA – Muslim Businessmen Association
MYNA – Muslim Youth of North America
IFC – Isna Fiqh committee
IPAC – Isna Political Awareness Committee
IED – Islamic Education Department
MAYA – Muslim Arab Youth Association
MISG – Muslim Islamic Study Group
IAP – Islamic Association of Palestine
UASR – United Association for Studies and Research
OLF – Occupied Land Fund
MIA – Mercy International Association
ICNA – Islamic Circle of North America
BME – Baitul Mal Inc
IIIT – International Institute for Islamic Thought
IIC – Islamic Information Center
CAIR – Council on American-Islamic Relations
End of Memorandum.